Dad, Win Without
A Lawyer
While Rediscovering Your Soul

CAREY LINDE

Chi3tmas 2016

Dale This baby would have
been still born without you.
forever gratefull
Carey

DEDICATION

To those men, and the women who love them, that trusted me
with their children in a rigged game. We are all kin.

DISCLAIMER

TABLE OF CONTENTS

AUTHOR'S NOTE

Reading back over a trove of college scrap books and journals from the wild and wonderful '60s, I recognize the practical idealism of a Vermont Yankee that has sustained me from the heights of the Himalayas to the valleys of grief. From my current vantage point, I am in balance. But what am I to do with this bastard child handbook that has been fermenting for decades in the root cellar of my mind? Hand maidens of the global father's movement have forced me to the operating table. They demand I consent to the immediate uncorking of that vintage barrel that is my unedited, roughly hewn, politically incorrect, thoughts on a book (a book that was originally dreamt up decades ago to expense trips to visit with the Dalai Lama in India and around the world). If I don't put the book up for its immediate adoption, some sort of an elephant's graveyard awaits where all well-intentioned lawyers end up.

Under pressure from without and within, I offer up what I have in unfinished rag tag form. Into a skillet on a stove heated by the issues of the day are mixed as wide a variety of healthy common sense from any garden nourished with love. Out comes what I hope will be, if not recognized as proper food to some people's taste, a good enough omelet for a hungry father.

For two summers in my early college years I waited tables in a fashionable rustic Vermont country inn, The Inn at Weston. Chris, the bartender, had a jug behind his bar into which the last drops of every emptied bottle were poured. At the end of the night those who cared could sample the resulting concoction. This book is a similar mixture of spirits.

Please accept what you find in this book as coming from a member of the audience suddenly asked to give an impromptu speech. He reaches within himself and stutters out a last-minute assembly of ideas that have been playing billiards in his skull for decades.

Volumes have been written on the subjects lightly touched upon in this book. The broad nature of the subject and an understanding of its multifaceted dynamics allows for only the briefest of commentary. Many more insights, topics and tips could be added. This book is the proverbial tip of the iceberg of psychological and legal practice help for self-representing fathers. My objective is to point the reader in the right direction. If I can spark an interest to want to learn more, I have succeeded.

I have created a companion website, www.dadwinwithoutalawyer.com, where I will place more detailed and in-depth articles and connections to similar sites.

It is my sincerest desire that what you learn from this book will not only help you at the present moment in your life, but will serve has a beacon for years to come.

Readers are invited to submit thoughts, reactions, criticisms and their own stories for our edited blog www.divorce-for-men.com. Tips of practice from lawyers are welcome.

Fast Eddie: You sure don't leave much when you miss, do you, Fats?

Minnesota Fats: That's what the game's all about.

\- *The Hustler*

Sincerely,
Carey Linde

INTRODUCTION

*"All happy families are like one
another; each unhappy family is unhappy
in its own way." – Tolstoy, from the first
sentence in Anna Karenina.*

I'm sorry that you find yourself reading this book. Most likely, the reason is that your life has been turned upside down and you are in a state of shock, confusion, and panic because the one person in whose hands you placed your trust and love has now become your adversary. The most important point I hope to make is that your struggle with your former lover and the co-parent of your child must be separated from your primary duty as a parent: your love for your children. As misguided as you think it is, they need their mother's love as well as yours.

While I hope to give you information that will help you on your legal journey, my goal is to offer a guide to help you not just to survive the legal process. The main goal is to suggest how you can become a more creative, purposeful, compassionate, and happier person and father after the litigation is behind you.

Whether you have just separated from the mother of your children and the court process is ahead of you, or you are in the court process now, or this life-changing event is behind you, my message is the same: vigorously grasp this dark passage on the path of your life as an unequaled opportunity to shed your misconceived hero ideal. We all have dreams. When they shatter, letting go of illusions can be the most difficult and painful part. While the practical realities of the battle you are facing might dominate your thoughts right now, this book suggests that there is something more important to be learned. That lesson is not about betrayal, though betrayal may be the thing keeping you up at night. It urges you instead to look deep into yourself and rediscover the soul you have ignored for too long.

Every misfortune is an opportunity in disguise. I hope to take you on a journey that will not only make you a stronger person in court but a stronger person in life and a better parent because of the pain you've faced and overcome.

"That which doesn't kill me makes me stronger". - Nietzsche

The strategies, tactics, and tips in this book come from many decades litigating in the gauntlets of court, negotiating on courthouse steps, and mediating disputes. For you, this is probably your first time in court, making it harder to separate your anger and your pain from navigating the ordeal you are facing. But you must. Men who wish to remain an active part of their children's lives must remember that they want to spare their children from pain. To do so they have to become stronger and better than they have ever been. You can too. Dig deep, deeper than the source of the pain. There you will find yourself.

When you walk into the courtroom, it must be with a mental attitude imbued with self-knowledge, enabling you to put aside the pain, losses, and failures so that you can become the father your child needs.

When all hell has broken loose in your life, is a unique time to take a measure of your life. For a father, there is no hell worse than the gut wrenching fear of losing his children to an ex lying to the courts, her lawyer, her family, and herself. Lacking the resources to have a good lawyer intensifies that fear. You are entitled to feel crippled, lost in confusion, and helpless. You must and can conquer it.

The good news is that your situation can be transformed into a unique opportunity to analyze your life, your marriage, and how you arrived at where you are. You are now free to assess what you need to do without delusions and to come out at the end of it all a healthier, more self-aware person. Best of all, if you take this journey, you will be a better father and the courts will notice. The easy response to injustice is to just react, to adopt a defensive position, to fall into an attitude expected of you by your attacker. That is a mistake many men make. Most certainly you need to focus on your defense of parental rights, but you can do that while designing an effective offensive position.

Success in family court requires more than a clever legal strategy: it requires a healthy body and mind. This most simple of truths is the easiest to overlook, particularly when your whole world is collapsing. You can have good facts and evidence on your side, but without emotional stability and your eye on the correct ball, the court biases against fathers and the maneuvers of opposing lawyers can keep you from your children. Because you really only get one good kick at the legal "can," it is absolutely critical you bring your very best game to court. Key to being at the top of your game is emotional stability, conviction of purpose, positive energy, and a respect for the role of the mother in your child's life.

If you are only reading this book for legal jargon and tactics, then it may not do well in your case. This a not a game of who is smarter or trickier. This is a test of who is a good parent – not the best parent. Only a good enough parent. Good parents are mentally stable and present themselves as such in court.

A father came in to my office seeking help years ago. He was justifiably upset at how the system was allowing his vindictive ex-wife to keep his children from him with false allegations. After hearing his story, I was concerned that his degree of anger might be a detriment to his moving forward in the legal process. However, he seemed in sufficient control of his emotions after we discussed some strategies and ideas for exposing the mother's falsehoods. He was somehow familiar to me. I asked him if we had ever met before. Yes, he told me. He had come in to see me three years earlier. I had refused to act for him because his anger was out of control. I had told him to go and get good therapy and then come back. He took my advice and came back prepared to walk out onto the playing field.

This book, though written for fathers, can also be of use to women who may find themselves in the same predicament. Outside of the courtroom, neither gender has a monopoly on being the most suitable parent. Inside the courtroom, this equal playing ground often doesn't manifest. To the courts it is the child, and not the parent, who's rights are of primary concern. The primary goal of a judge should be to grant equal access to both parents so the child may benefit from the well-rounded nurture and guidance of the mother and father. Unfortunately, fathers find themselves subject to myths about mothers being the more loving and emotionally connected parent and face a bias that starts them out on unequal footing. As a father, you need to be prepared to face this challenge with confidence and perseverance.

For fathers, the first part of the court battle is to do the necessary groundwork to prepare yourself psychologically. Preparedness of your person and mind is essential to success in court and the first part of this book devotes significant attention to how you might navigate that journey. Make no mistake, the personal work suggested in this book is essential not only for your emotional well-being and that of your child, but is absolutely required for you to improve your child's chances of keeping you in their life.

The second part deals primarily with your ex, how her thought process will likely work, and what you can expect to encounter from her and her lawyer.

In parts three and four, I explore the basics of family law, rules of court, and procedures that you'll have to become familiar with. People who are unfamiliar with the court system and its unique approach to problem solving may struggle to make sense of why the rules are set the way they are and how to express themselves within those guidelines. I hope to provide you with some of the necessary tools and tips for court, how to deal with your ex and her lawyer, and tactics you can apply to the specific needs of your case.

Some of what you read may seem like pop psychology.

While you might feel it is all very interesting stuff, you are in the middle of a life shattering experience that demands your full attention. Discussions about finding your inner self, your soul, while all well and good, can damned well wait!

Fair enough. But not only can you do both types of learning at once, you must. What may seem like steps you'd take in post-trial recovery are actually the skills essential to have under your belt the moment you walk up the courthouse steps.

Every great tradition throughout the history of mankind tells us that the very best opportunities to acquire deep self-awareness come in the chaos of life's most difficult experiences. That is the test you face right now. Few events in the life of a man are more disastrous than the loss of the relationship with the mother of his children, especially where that mother seeks to minimize or deny him a relationship with his children. Few times in one's life are more opportune for self-reflection and growth. It is a rare man, who hearing wise voices from the past, undertakes the arduous and seemingly impossible journey to find the path of rediscovery of the man he could yet become. Because you have found your way to this, and other similar books, you may be such a man.

Fathers whose former partners are reasonable women, who value and support his relationship with their children, only have to deal with the grieving period to overcome the death of the marriage. That is hard enough, but nowhere near the nightmare of fearing they are going to lose their children to her. They have time to devote their battered energies to regrowth, to getting on, and to work on the new relationship and reality with their children. Not having to constantly fight a rearguard action against a vindictive mother set on denying them their children is a luxury for such men.

Such men can more easily focus their attention on their own steps forward. They can make space in their daily lives for the cultivation of positive and growth-oriented moments. Their efforts at finding their new path are unobstructed by their former partner. Their mood is not burdened by the soul killing fear of losing their children. And most critically of all, their daily energies and all their financial capacity aren't overcome with having to fight the legal system that favors mothers over fathers. For such fortunate men, the chance to be a fundamentally happier person for the rest of his life, and thereby better co-parent his children, is real and tangible. This book is for less fortunate men.

The father who must fight on behalf of his children not only has this emotional challenge, he has the added hell of lawyers, courtrooms and, for some, the daily fear of yet another false allegation. Fending off attacks, fighting just to hold his ground, mortgaging his last possession, and losing past friends can become a destructive obsession that eats away at his self-esteem and mental stability. For him, to dedicate part of his daily routine to improving his self-awareness and working on being a happier and healthier person seems like a luxury he can't afford. Or at least that is what he thinks. In that thought, he is wrong.

For many men going through litigation it is often the first time in their lives they have not had at least some sense of control over every aspect of their lives. Having the legal system take away that control can be a really frightening experience. Trapped in a legal system that does not have his best interests at heart and in a society that believes women over men, fathers find themselves facing judges who think women are to be believed and are inherently better able to nurture and raise children than men.

The courtroom, with the presiding judge raised up above all others is a daunting, often fearful place for most people at first. Even for lawyers, sometimes succeeding in court takes more than just skill, it takes some luck. Self-represented fathers have something no lawyer can have: the full history, sincerity, heart, and their love for their child. The father need only acquire an understanding of the theatrical nature of the process, the roles each person plays, and the stage upon which they perform their lines. Many different prepared and rehearsed scripts get heard each day in family courts. The scripts which work for fathers are ones in which they stand up for their children's rights, seeking equal time and opportunity in their lives. They all share certain common themes. The most successful approach is to acknowledge the mother's role as a parent, while fighting for the same respect.

Success in family court requires a man to be the type of person the judge wants him to be. Judges have set ideas about who deserves to remain in the lives of their children. If you walk into the courtroom insincere, not having become the person in your script, it may be easily seen through and have the opposite effect. The goal is to find and bring your authentic self into harmony with your environment. When you are genuine, your voice will be heard loud and clear. There will be no need to shout. The courtroom is not a place to fake it.

Rather than begrudge and resist the legal process, fathers need to see it as an unequaled opportunity. Why? Because there is a strong and important relationship between the character role you must learn to play for the stage of the courtroom and the renewed person you hope to eventually become once this is all behind you. The persona you adopt for the legal process can be made into an excellent practice run at eventually finding your own path of self-discovery. You don't need to be trapped in the legal process. You can let it defeat you, or you can take what little control is available and learn to master it.

The mothers described in this book represent that minority of personality-disordered women whose intransigence to reason makes them over-represented in family   court.

PART I – HEALING YOURSELF

CHAPTER 1:   A FOOL FOR A CLIENT

There is a saying that a man who represents himself in court has a fool for a client. Don't believe it! It doesn't have to be true. The legal profession, as all other professions, has successfully propagandized the general public that only their licensed members have the skills required. However, the warning applies to some professions, such as medicine, much more than to law. You wouldn't want to perform your own heart surgery. However, you sure can do a good job – perhaps the best – speaking on behalf of your own children. That voice speaks the truth.

Fathers and mothers are representing themselves in family courts in record numbers inundating the system. Courts everywhere are moving to accommodate this phenomenon. Join the crowd!

"Foolishness" is representing yourself without first doing homework. Obviously a very basic understanding on family law and procedure can only help. It is not all that difficult. The basic rules are simple and logical.

I have written this book to help single fathers improve their own self-awareness and thus be better able to master the simple skills required to represent themselves in court. The self-awareness, and the emotional control that comes with it, must precede or occur jointly with learning the rules of the game. And it is a game, with special rules on its own playing filed. Separated mothers in court, up against control freak fathers of their children, should also benefit from this book.

A benefit to representing yourself in family court is strategic: lawyers are required to act in court according to strict rules. Key among the rules in interim applications is the one that prohibits lawyers from alleging facts that have not previously been sworn to in an affidavit or revealed in discovery or deposition. Unrepresented fathers aren't expected to fully appreciate that fact. Judges often let them tell their story in their own words, with their own real emotions, letting in facts or argument a lawyer could not. No lawyer can inject the full human impact of what the father is going through.

Judges make an extra effort to see that unrepresented parents understand what is happening in their courtrooms. They often protect the parent from an aggressive or unethical lawyer on the other side. I have seen fathers who weren't getting from the courts what they wanted, left their lawyers, represented themselves, and then the court gave them what they wanted. It happens. You can do it.

The Myth of Dead Beat Dads

In 40 years of family law, I have never met a dead-beat dad, if by "dead beat" one means a father who willfully and with intent is underemployed for the sole purpose of avoiding child support. What I have seen are legions of fathers whose changing circumstances prevent them from earning what they would like to. Various heartless agencies of government and their legal hyenas pursue these men with a blood-thirsty vengeance, seizing driver's licenses and passports.

What I have seen are untold numbers of mothers manufacturing elaborate excuses why they can't get a job even as a waitress because the children need them to be home, or they want the father to foot the bill for schooling to become a counselor to help women like themselves abused by men.

Are there father's out there willfully underemployed? Some. Are there mothers out there who kill their newborns and leave them in a dumpster? Some. But we don't call them dumpster moms.

A common mantra from personality-disordered mothers is that the father's sole purpose in seeking more time with the children is to get out of having to pay as much child support. I have had many father clients offer to maintain full child support to the mother regardless as to the time he parents the children. Women are now fully in the workforce.   But   dads   are   still   the   wallet.

CHAPTER 2:   THE HERO MENTALITY

"In the middle of the path through life

I suddenly found myself in a dark wood."

Dante, Divine Comedy.

The first, and most difficult, challenge that you will face now that your life has been turned upside down is to restore your equilibrium. Until this point, you have lived by setting goals, planning the accomplishment of those goals and celebrating each one as you reached it. Things have changed. All of your hard-won successes have been ripped away. Even your identity may have been stolen from you. Instead of the stoic pillar of wisdom and stability you envisioned, you are a tattered sail blowing on the mast of a sunken ship. Instead of the hero you sought to be, you find yourself painted the villain.

Nothing is a harder taskmaster in teaching us that the only constant in life is change than the loss of a loving relationship. The loss of a relationship with the mother of your children brings with it collateral damage to all aspects of your life. It particularly threatens the relationship with your children and how they view you as a father.

No one has articulated your present position in life better than Jungian Psychologist James Hollis:

"One of the most powerful shocks of the
Middle Passage is the collapse of our tacit
contract with the universe - the
assumption that if we act correctly, if we
are of good heart and intentions, things

will work out. We assume a reciprocity with the universe. If we do our part the universe will comply. Many ancient stories, including the Book of Job, painfully reveal the fact that there is no such contract, and everyone who goes through the Middle Passage is made aware of it. No one sets out upon the marital barque, for example, without high hopes and good intentions, however uncertain the compass and shifting the tides. When one stands amid the rubble of a partnership, then one has not only lost the relationship, but also, the whole world view."
- James Hollis, The Middle Passage: From Misery to Meaning in Midlife.

Your innate sense of reciprocity and fairness will meet many challenges before you emerge at the other end of the divorce courts. One of the toughest pills to swallow is this: bad people don't always get their just deserts. You may think a court of law will shine a light on lies and right injustices but, by the end, you'll probably feel that any justice achieved happened despite the courts not because of them. You are not Superman any more. You are more like Clark Kent with no phone booth.

Hero Mentality
Today's fathers grew up as boys measuring themselves and their dreams against the "heroes" projected before them by the mass media culture of their youth: cowboys, astronauts, firemen, or Steve Jobs. Parents, school and society told us we could become whatever we wanted. As

these boys became adolescents, they found that those same parents, schools and voices of society narrowed the boundaries of what we should or shouldn't seek to become. The idealized childhood hero we imagined was encroached upon bit by bit until our dreams were distorted to accommodate expectations and maturing realities. Our self-definition, our soul, are sacrificed on the altar of conformity.

The process by which our environment narrows down our options and desires and dictates what we decide to become as adults is the same process that stops us from developing other more satisfying visions of ourselves. This funneling effect of your goals inhibits or prevents the development of spirit and joy; concepts and goals given very little weight in that same environment.

As we grow, we modify our hero ambitions into something a bit more "practical", but the hero ideal persists. We reset our sights on a practical choice of job or profession. These dreams are supplanted and replaced, directing us to aspire to be a good husband and father, sharing an exciting life with an ideal woman. In the past, for young men, they bought into the dream of finding the right person to have children with and becoming the very best parent the world has ever seen. The dangling carrot of love turns previously uncommitted young men into warriors of their dreams. Socrates said that love is the hunger of the human soul for divine beauty. This is the young man's hero quest. When you father a child, that quest deepens in meaning and intensity.

Within the current breakdown of the structures that used to support marriage as an institution, too many men, after years of devoting all their energy to be a good husband and father, find it has unraveled and the dream of being a hero to their child turns into a nightmare.

No cultural foundation comes with as much expectations and baggage as the institution of marriage, and parenthood. This particular institution has been so deeply rooted in our society that few are ever really aware of the full range of demands it makes upon us. This is particularly true at this moment in history when the very concept of family and the role of men and women within it are changing. This is truer for fathers whose gender roles can become blurred with increasing numbers of mothers in the workplace and fathers in the home (or wanting to be more in the home).

The expectations of marriage and parenthood all too frequently come crashing down against the reality that the only constant is change. Any fixed ideas that there could ever be permanence in any relationship are out the window. An early victim to the break-up of the relationship with the mother of your children is the very masculine instinct and perception that you could protect your children from exactly what you now know is about to descend upon them.

American author and philosopher Henry David Thoreau once said "the mass of men lead lives of quiet desperation, and go to the grave with the song still in them." When you find yourself in a divorce, the relationship which once seemed to you a joining of souls that held darkness at bay becomes a magnifying glass on a quiet desperation that lurked beneath the surface. This hidden sadness is something only seen in hindsight because, in your current state, all meaning the relationship once gave to your life has been stripped away. You'll find yourself doubting everything you thought you knew about this woman you once loved. Even worse, you'll find that you now doubt yourself. How could you have been so fooled?

Some men spend the remainder of their lives blaming themselves. Others, blind to the realities of their true situation, struggle to maintain their illusion of the hero dream. Even though these men eventually come to know that it was a false dream in the first place, they are too fearful to abandon it, holding onto it even tighter. Your ex-wife has no such delusions. The judge has no such delusions. The proper approach to successful communication will have to fall in the middle ground. Stop blaming yourself for what you couldn't control but don't present yourself as the superhero with all the answers. You need to negotiate and come to the table as a rational person.

Leave your personal mythology behind. It was a dream never capable of bringing happiness into your life. False dreams are what led to the collapse of your relationship. Wherever your future goes, it needs to be grounded in reality and based on goals that reflect your new-found needs. Only a few men acquire the insight – usually through some life tragedy – to grasp the incredible opportunity to abandon their hero dream and permit the rebirth of their soul. You have that chance now.

The term "midlife crisis" is over-used in sitcoms and pop magazines to describe a wide range of minor and major problems we face as we head into our '40s or later. However, it is undeniable that men come up against a predictable pattern of serious problems in mid-life. Nasty new truths suddenly appear on the horizon of your life. One of them is a spiffy lawyer eager to help your ex-wife strip you of all your worth. Profound changes occur. They work their way into your mind, challenging your old truths. No longer does the virtue of having lived a good and honest life guarantee just outcomes.

This book is for those men whose relationship with the mother of their children has been shattered on the rocky shoals of life; who are now ready to abandon their failed hero dreams in favor of swimming to a new shore on the strength of their undiscovered inner selves.

If you assume that the causes for the collapse of your dreams exist outside of yourself (i.e. it's your wife's fault or someone else's fault), then you are probably doomed to repeat it all over again with the next woman who stirs your loins. If, on the other hand, you can own up to the possibility that there was something misguided within yourself that contributed to it all, there is hope.

To not only survive but to come out of this stage in your life as a truly healthier and happier person, you need to turn to teachers. Ours is a curious society in which we think only children need teachers, although in recent times there is a fad of new age spirituality and soul searching that is largely fueled by women toting yoga mats under their arms. The type of soul I talk about in this book is not the alleged immortal soul of religion. It is your essence. It is the root of who you really are under all the labels others have pinned on you.

For older men, the cultural ethic was that after high school, trade school, or college, each of us was on our own, self-sufficient, and any need for further guidance was seen as a weakness. It is survival of the fittest. One of the shocks of mid-life is the discovery that we seem to have few tools to help us when facing emotional turbulence. We need to look for teachers we can trust. This search for guidance can build your inner voice or intuition. When you search out books, groups, or mentors, look for men and women who have been where you now find yourself but sample their advice before you buy it wholesale. Look for guides who have worked through their own emotional wounds, and their own challenges and who speak in a voice that you connect with. Don't shape yourself into their vision of the perfect you. Find people who can help you to start living by your own vision. Don't accept another's version of who you are. Find the guide who will help you discovery yourself.

There are parts to this book and some of my advice that may not connect with your unique situation. I can only tell you what I have experienced in my own life and from my work over the years helping children see more of their parents, mainly fathers.

Some of what I say may seem a little melodramatic to your particular situation. However, if the courts are about to pull off a judicial kidnapping of your children, don't let it drive you crazy. You can beat the biased system by being a stronger, more disciplined, patient, and better person.

CHAPTER 3:   THE NECESSITY OF PATIENCE

*"What we need is a cup of
understanding, a barrel of love, and an
ocean of patience." - St. Francis de Sales.*

Patience, more than almost any other skill, is an absolute requirement for a father coming out of a failed relationship. Patience is a critical discipline for success in family law and part of that discipline is gauging when to act and when to wait.

The time to act is early, if not immediately. Initially, leading up to and just after separation, a man can be too patient, caused by timidity, fear, uncertainty, or sometimes just being too nice a guy. Fathers, more often than mothers, are more eager to keep the family unit together. We have no statistics on how successful such individuals are but we have lots of statistics on how many fathers end up losing legal ground, their home, and their children due to stoic patience and lack of early action.

When a father fears separation from his children, both physically and emotionally, he experiences a mental tug of war between his heart and his mind. His heart urges patience and consideration, time and space to try and work things out. If he still loves his wife and she is the one who left, he puts the hope of reconciliation at the top of his priorities. Still in disbelief, many men resist abandoning hope of reconciliation creating a dangerous denial of their precarious position. Meanwhile, the mind is warning in loud, obnoxious blasts against delay in seeking legal advice before he is locked out and stuck peering in on the life of his children from the outside.

This is a book for men who can't afford lawyers. That being said, if you can scrape together some money, enough for a lawyer to do just one thing for you, do the following or find out how to do it yourself: Commence a court action right away and get a court order to secure the best initial position you can with respect to time with your children. This is normally called an access or parenting order and you can't afford delay. From the beginning, a legal fence needs to be constructed around any ambitions the mother might have to minimize the father's access. While you wait, the mother is establishing "facts on the ground." The longer she acts as the primary parent, with limited access for you, the more difficult it will be for a judge to disrupt the status quo. Slippage must be arrested. If your parenting time is being denied or limited, you need to arrest any further erosion before it becomes the norm. Once you have accomplished this important step, you must settle in for the long haul. Patience must now become your constant companion.

When seeking an order granting the most optimal parenting schedule for the children at that moment, make sure the order states that it is interim or temporary subject to review in the future. Without this codicil, you may not be able to challenge the existing order unless there is a material change of circumstances or an expensive trial.

As soon as a father sees an attempt by the mother to change the relationship between himself and his children, he should consult a lawyer if possible. Under no circumstances should he remain complacent. There should be no patience and delay on this point. No giving in to any appeal by the mother for the father to accept such a change on any temporary or experimental basis "for the sake of the children." "Why don't you go and stay at your brother's for just a little while to give the children and me some space to try and work things out?" More doors have been shut against fathers with those sorts of seductive pleas than by any other. Don't buy into it. Suggest maybe she go stay with her mother and leave you and kids in the home.

Once armed with even minimal court protection, you must prepare for the long court struggle ahead. Once a legal beachhead as been established, it is time to back away and gather your strength. Fathers must become very patient over the next several months or years of working through the legal system. Type-A personalities are in for a new kind of shock. The court process is a challenge to anyone's definition of efficient and speedy process. Welcome to the world of molasses.

The name of the game in normal everyday working life is thrift, efficiency, timeliness, reasonableness, and effort rewarded by results. The experience for fathers in family law is delay, frustration, irrationality, more delay, experts with little time to do what they are asked, serious efforts often producing little or nothing, more delay, and a constant uphill struggle against the many vestiges of gender bias.

Men who have spent years mastering technical problems, who can be successful under the most difficult of work circumstances, who can efficiently do what has to be done in a life-and-death emergency, who can put together the most complicated of business deals under extreme time restraints – such men can become frustrated beyond belief in the tediously drawn out, grossly inefficient and very expensive family law system. For a father who makes his living through physical work in a wage job, his life's lessons taught and learned are equally turned upside down. Having to navigate through the psychological, procedural, and legal minefields of divorce can be the worst experience in a man's life.

Most courthouses provide free legal advice on how to prepare and file court applications. Some provide limited free, or pro bono legal advice from lawyers available on site. Warning! Don't let the lawyer talk you out of what you believe to be right. Most family lawyers are good on defense and bad on offence.

After getting advice from a lawyer, the same mental tug-of-war remains. One side of the intellectual game being played in your head says, "Do we negotiate? Would going to court ruin any chance of a negotiated settlement? Would taking legal action merely get her mad? Will it forever doom any chance of us ever getting back together?"

These are always important questions that need to be carefully examined. Being too patient here can allow the mother to solidify her position and slowly but certainly chip away at the children's time and rights with their father. If you are an "every other weekend and Wednesday afternoon" father hoping she will see the light and give you more time, every week you delay taking action can work against you and bolster the mother's position.

Again, being patient here can prove to be a fatal mistake. If the facts of the case require a court action to be started, if for no other purpose than to "freeze" the situation and halt the further erosion of the children's position with their father, it should be done. Doing so never prevents the parties from continuing negotiations. Where parties have not been negotiating before legal action, they often then start to. Experienced lawyers should leave the door open for negotiations at all times. Having said this, the fact that you are reading this book may suggest that negotiations are a naive hope at best, and at worst a waste of time and money. If negotiations are ever going to work, the most effective time frame is just before the trial is to commence. While it is obviously desirable for parents to resolve their problems with as little conflict as possible, men reading this book are probably not dealing with a woman who is acting reasonably or even rationally.

Judges need to be shown a great deal of evidence to conclude that a mother is not acting reasonably. They may make statements asserting that they assume both sides are reasonable loving parents. If you present your case aggressively with an attitude of assigning blame and anger any perceived animosity to the situation will default to blame the father. You can't just tell a judge that you, the father, are the reasonable person. You must present the judge with evidence that demonstrates her unreasonableness. That is where patience and self-awareness become important. If she is paranoid, don't say so. Show how she is paranoid. Then say something like: "I am not a psychologist, but it seems to me she might be paranoid."

Once having made the decision to start legal proceedings, or having been forced to defend yourself, "patience" takes on a whole new meaning. This is true not only in terms of the tactics required to maximize success in the legal action, but also in terms of the psychology of the parties involved.

Patience as a Tactic in Legal Proceedings

One of the most misunderstood family court rules is this: once an order has been made by a judge on a certain matter, it is very difficult to change it – often impossible – until and unless there has been a major change in the circumstances surrounding the issue the order addresses, or until there can be a full trial on the issue. In practical terms, this means that you don't lightly go into court without a well thought out strategy but, if you have to, seek limited goals that leave open the opportunity to come back for larger gains once you are better prepared.

Many family law disputes in the courts settle early, some for the right reasons and some for the wrong reasons. There are always some that become really nasty, driven by an anger and selfishness that is hard to comprehend. In these cases, no detail large or small can be worked out without a fight.

Mothers like this fall into a broad spectrum of conflict-oriented personalities. They are frequently passive aggressive, borderline, or bi-polar. Such a mother frequently resorts to false or exaggerated allegations of abuse or harassment to gain greater sympathy from the courts, her lawyer, and any health care professionals involved. Such women often plot and provoke an incident so they can call the police, or retreat to a women's shelter. Sometimes the husband responds in the heat of the moment, totally out of character, in an inappropriate way. The cops come and the wife gets a restraining order against him. If it was just an issue between two people who once loved each other that would be one thing The real harm being done is that the mother will use these incidents as excuses to get the court to restrict access or completely remove the father from the lives of the children.

This most abusive and damaging act against the children by the mother is often hypocritically justified by her and her lawyer as being "in the best interests of the children." It is really her own interests that are being served. A significant part of that self-interest is always financial: custody of children means money, pure and simple. Of that there can be no debate.

Clients who come to lawyers in this situation have an added difficulty of getting back into the lives of their children. The scales have to be put back into balance and only when the pendulum is back in the center can one begin to try and repair things. A great amount of patience is required during this often long and lonely process. Responding too aggressively may backfire and cause a judge to mistake your pain as confirmation of an anger disorder.

There are no magic cures or slam dunks available in family law when a mother sets out to fracture the relationship between her children and their father. The process is very time consuming and only with "an ocean of patience" can you see it through. You must learn to stay steadfast in your character and focused on your own sense of identity, which cannot be stolen by lies. This is the core of why you must spend as much time, if not more, on your inner work as you do on dealing with the legal paperwork and strategies. It is not just your resources that are under attack but your very identity. Remember that your bitter ex-wife no longer gets to control who you are. That's the good part of getting divorced.

Patience as a Required Mental Discipline
Twenty-five hundred years ago, Sun Tzu, a Chinese Taoist warrior, wrote the first, and some still say the best, book on war: *The Art of War*. Some of Sun Tzu's wisdom:

- "The best way to win a war is the complete and total surrender of the enemy before he mounts a defense."

- "To defeat the enemy psychologically is superior to beating him militarily. "

- "To win without fighting is best. "

- "If compassionate toward yourself, you can reconcile the world. "

- "Skillful warriors first make themselves invincible and await the enemies' vulnerability. "

- "The defender must know one's self. "

- "When strong, appear weak. When weak, appear strong. "

- "All war is based on deception."

- "Feign inferiority to encourage your enemy's arrogance. By appearing lowly and weak, you allow your enemy to let down his guard."

Try to understand these quotes as structural supports or rewards for your own developing inner patience. Only then can the psychological truths contained in those quotes be put into a sustained practice. Also, keep in mind that your enemy may be using the same tactics.

Acting on your own without a lawyer allows you to "feign inferiority" in a very creative fashion. Play dumb to the mother's lawyer. Feed their arrogance. Let the lawyer and the mother think they have you over a barrel. In such cases, they may put statements in writing to you that demonstrate that arrogance. If the mother has personality disorders that are hard to bring to the service for the world to see, they often show their nature when they think they can attack you because you are down.

Dynamics of Patience vs Procrastination

There is an important difference between patience and procrastination. While patience is your greatest virtue once engaged with the legal process, procrastination is a vice. Procrastinating means putting off to a later time something that should be done right away. Impatience is attempting to do something right away that should be put off to a later time. Understanding the distinction between these two dynamics is difficult for a man trying to deal with a collapsing relationship. A "push me-pull you" force tugs you in opposite directions. You hope that if you ignore the selfish demands being made of you by your child's mother they will simply go away, but god damn it, if she makes one more demand you are going to let her know what you think!

Life is full of mixed messages and apparent contradictions. Many people in an unraveling relationship struggle with these opposing forces. It is hard to be patient when the walls are falling down around you, yet, like a deer stuck in the headlights, we sometimes freeze in procrastination, refusing to take action and rationalizing it by telling ourselves we are not capable of anything at the moment.

It may be tempting to mislabel your procrastination as an act of patience in order to excuse the behavior. Learn the difference and find ways to push yourself through any tasks that you've been stalling or mentally blocking yourself from following through on.

Procrastinating is passive, the doing of nothing for avoidance purposes. Patience, as Confucius said, is not passive but on the contrary, is a concentrated strength. Strength is what you need now, in spades.

If needed, get help in finding out what underlying blockage you have preventing you from making decisions. Perhaps it is fear of making a mistake or you have some sort of perfectionism problem worried about not doing something perfectly. It could be residue from you earlier heroic sense of self not wanting to upset people or cause stress to family members. Or perhaps you think taking action is a sign of caving in to doing what someone else wants you to do. Deal with it. Your real self-worth will ultimately be discovered by how creatively and openly you tackle, overcome, and get beyond this stage in your life. The concern over what others think of you, some of which will have been tainted by lies about you, will not be solved by continuing to let other people's opinions define your sense of self.

In the end, you are the one who owns your identity. No matter what others may have said about you, they are not you. Only you get to decide who you are. Your knowledge of self is what matters and that is why you must become self-aware. The more in control you are of your own identity the more likely it is that a judge will see the "real" you and not the version of "you" your ex is trying to paint.

Patience, on the other hand, means living with things as they are until they can be changed. It means accepting the moment and choosing your actions carefully. It means having the strength to over-come frustration while waiting for the right moment for change. Patience requires forbearance while figuring out a better strategy. Being patient in a situation of hardship does not mean doing nothing to improve things. Accept the truth of the moment and try to find peace while you wait for better times.

Learn to Recover Patience

No matter how rambunctious you might have been as a child, there is probably at least one cherished memory of sitting in stillness and feeling connected to the world. A feature of childhood is the lack of control you have over the circumstances of your life. Where you live, where you attend school, which adults have governance over your daily routines, how your home is structured, is all controlled by the adults who rule over you. Even in the midst of that environment, you were able to sit in the world and find moments of quiet and peace.

When I try and recall the moments in my life when I first experienced total contentment in the present moment, unfettered with concerns of the past or the future, they all involve being in nature.

The earliest of such memories is at age 5 or 6 near my

home in central rural Massachusetts. It was a warm summer day and I was sitting under the overhanging branches of a white pine looking out onto a small clearing in the tranquil woods. I can still smell the sun on the soft carpet of dried pine needles that surrounded me. A mother grouse ever so cautiously stepped out from the undergrowth into the warm clearing. She was soon followed by a parade of very young chicks. How long they remained before me, how long I was one with that very special world, I do not know. It may have been merely minutes or it could have been an hour. For me, as for the grouse and the trees, time literally stood still. Only the moment had meaning.

A few years later, I would enjoy walking across fields and streams up to a pasture on a hill below another woods in Vermont. Just before the tree line a fox had dug a den. I spent many fine late afternoons sitting for hours on end, just waiting. I was oblivious to the human world and the demands it made upon young boys. Eventually, at sunset, the mother fox and her young would carefully emerge from their home in the earth. Soon they would be frolicking in a world of their own that I felt totally connected to.

There were also many wonderful hours sitting by a beaver pond at dusk waiting for and then watching the beavers set about their industrious chores. Those were all experiences I gleefully sought out. Looking back at the dozens upon dozens of such escapades, I can see it was the sense of stillness and time forgotten that was the main attraction. Being one with Mother Nature. Long before psychedelics and the magic mushroom

There was another kind of experience that took more conscious learning to be still and patient. That was standing in a makeshift blind on a deer run in the woods during bow and arrow season in upper Michigan with my father. The better part of a whole day could be taken up with this forced inactivity. Eventually I learned to let my senses take in the activity surrounding us. I could be mesmerized for hours by the comings and goings of chipmunks, woodpeckers, rabbits, and even spiders and ants. Time would stand still.

These are all examples of patience, the skills I lost as an adult and that I am only now learning how to recover. It is not simple. But it is possible with mindfulness and meditation. Meditative patience may seem like an arduous task for a man in the middle of a nasty separation but if you seek this peace it will show in your face, in your eyes, and in your demeanor when you're in front of a judge.

Mindfulness is about finding that part of yourself that no one can take away.

"The greatest revelation is stillness." -
Lao-Tse

CHAPTER 4:   BECOMING THE NEW YOU

"I withdraw to a high vantage

To start anew....

The anger has past,

Now only remains calm.

Confusion replaced with conviction

That transitions are made

....pain with memories

....fear with understanding

....loneliness with vision

old joys with new beginnings." –
Anonymous

In the course of a relationship, bonds develop. The most obvious is love. With it comes the vulnerability of sharing your inner secrets and fragility with a person in a position of trust. Where that trust has been misplaced or the keeper of your life story has turned against you, betrayal and fear cripple your strength. Your adversary is now the person who has studied and learned all your weaknesses and who knows best how to penetrate your defenses.

In healthy relationships, each partner uses their knowledge of the other to enhance the relationship. In an unhealthy, coercive, or abusive relationship, one partner uses this knowledge, often unconsciously, to manipulate the other into playing a role in their fantasy. When a relationship fails, one partner may use this intimate knowledge to purposefully aggravate, injure, or control the other. Commonly, this is referred to as "pushing someone's buttons." This might manifest as a verbal slight meant to score a small, demoralizing victory. Or it could be a straight up provocation intended to get a physical response to justify calling the police.

Women are much more adept than men at knowing the other's buttons.

The best defense is to recognize and learn to control your weak areas or hot buttons. Figure them out and weld them shut. Practice having someone push the old buttons by getting a friend to role play or role play both sides yourself. You can go over memories of when your ex was able to elicit an emotional response and then replay the scenario letting yourself figure out ways to neutralize your reaction. You can't control other people but you can learn to control yourself. Learn to have no response. The next time she pushes that button and the expected response doesn't follow, she will feel jolted. She has lost something important to her: prediction, control and outcome.

Once We Were Kings (1996) is a great documentary directed by Leon Gast about Muhammad Ali and George Foreman, and their fight famously known as the Rumble in the Jungle. Ali won the title back by not boxing the way he had led Foreman to expect. Early right hand leads and the rope-a-dope during the middle rounds completely confounded Foreman.

The analogy is clear: when you have to engage with the legal system, don't be the target she is expecting and depending upon. Be something else. Be like Muhammad Ali and "float like a butterfly, sting like a bee."

When you find yourself losing the relationship you had with the mother of your children, it is normal to feel a certain amount of worry and guilt. We want to give our children the best chance at a successful, happy life experience. That means having a stable home with both parents. Evolutionary biology, subjected to societal and cultural controls, in this age of post capitalist industrialization has made this ethos of the two-parent home central to our culture. You are now seeking to find a creative solution to sustain and obtain stability and happiness outside of that model. Strip away the beliefs that don't serve you well or help with your situation then find a new way to support the underlying values of a two-parent family. For your children the two-parent family can work in two separated homes.

Children traditionally benefited from love and nurture from as many people as possible. Children were raised by a village. Modern society has narrowed the village down to pretty much just mom and dad. We have become a more isolated society, isolated from our communities. Many people couldn't tell you what their neighbor's names are. Their extended family members live in different cities. In North America, if a child is lucky, sometimes there is a grandparent, aunt or uncle who is regular part of their life because they live close by. In other cultures, children don't get raised exclusively by their biological parents. Extended members of the family are an active part of their home life. The important thing for you right now is that whatever time you have with your child will be spent lovingly. When your time becomes precious the role you play in that child's life becomes more meaningful. Your kids need their grandparents, on both sides. Aunts and uncles and cousins. As limited as your time with them may be, give up some of that precious time to your extended family.

Your children are going to have two homes, and receive as much nurture and love as possible in each of those homes. Rational mothers know this and support their children having two homes, encouraging bonds with each parent. Mothers with personality disorders, or who are emotionally imbalanced, are incapable of understanding this. That demographic, and their legal beagles still cling to the antiquated and destructive gender prejudice that Madam Justice Claire L'Heureux-Dube of the Supreme Court of

Canada had in mind when she said in Young v Young (1993) about fathers:

> *"The role of the access parent is that of a very interested observer giving love and support to the child in the background."*

About the custodial parent, she said:

> *"The need for continuity generally requires that the custodial parent have the autonomy to raise the child as he or she sees fit without interference with that authority by the . . . non-custodial parent."*

About the non-custodial parent, she said:

> *"...the non-custodial spouse with access privileges is a passive bystander who is excluded from the decision making process in matters relating to the child's welfare, growth and development."*

About men, she said:

> *"...men as a group have not yet embraced responsibility for childcare."*

While dysfunctional mothers see their world in those terms, the family courts have largely, but not entirely, come to accept and value the innate nurturing capacity of fathers and their vital contribution to the health of a child. Clearly and thankfully, Justice L'Heureux-Dube's notion of what fathers are capable of is and always was indisputably wrong.

Redefining the Concept of Home

Most of us were brought up believing that one home was the ideal. That is only true in a home which isn't in a constant state of conflict. In your new reality, you have to realize that your children can get all the benefits from one home doubled. Two good homes can provide more stability than one toxic home.

There are some disadvantages to split homes, such as extra financial burdens. Children who have two homes can learn to accommodate multiplicity and adapt to change in ways unavailable to a child living in a single, two-parent home. These skills give them an added benefit in their educational and working lives where variety and change have become more common in the modern workforce.

Another idea that needs to be deconstructed is the one we call "duty". Men are raised with a strong sense of obligation and duty to family. This initially starts out as duty to one's partner but grows into including duty toward children, and sometimes to one's extended elder family, which is then incorporated into a concept of family loyalty. This sense of duty has its pitfalls. Determination to meet this sense of duty can blind a man to the growing stresses, difficulties, and unhealthy family environment it may be reinforcing. When the family unit can no longer be salvaged, a father's primary duty is to himself and his children. Your choices should be based on what is best for your children, but also should include your own health and well-being so that you can be there for them body, heart, and mind.

Caring more for others than for yourself, particularly for your children, is an interesting altruist and moral idea. Staying in a relationship that is beyond repair out of some sense of duty is not good for anyone. Once you can extract yourself from that relationship, re-evaluate who and what you are in your life to come to better understand reality and your potential. You can then get on to dedicating yourself and energies towards others in a much more constructive and healthy way.

A big problem for some fathers is that the mothers of their children, having a well-honed understanding of the father's strengths and weaknesses, can manipulate a warrior-like sense of duty in a man. At best, it can cause confusion in the man, and at worst it will bring shame. Women are better at shaming than men. Women who do this, more often than not, are attempting to seek continuing support for their own emotional and psychological unmet needs at the expense of the man's. It is a very subtle process. This shaming is emotional abuse pure and simple.

The man who is the target of emotional abuse rarely appreciates the extent to which he has been psychologically crippled and entrapped by a modern definition of relationship that favors mothers over fathers. The end result is that your relationship and sense of self-worth has been dictated by the mother of your children. For men in this situation, they should abandon all hope of ever reconciling with their ex and build a support group that can help identify and correct the low self-esteem that has been ingrained. Usually we find that, once a toxic relationship has ended, our friends and family are relieved and say they had noticed it long ago. These people can help by giving you more accurate mirrors of your identity than the bad actor your ex is trying to paint. Once you realize how long you have allowed yourself to be abused, it is your obligation to identify and strengthen yourself against the insecurities that allowed it to happen. The emotional blackmail must end.

Fear of disapproval from others is a strong glue binding an unhealthy relationship together. Fear of disapproval of your partner, as ironic as it may be, also hinders some men from a healthy extraction from an unhealthy relationship. For men, worth is often assessed in society by the happiness of your wife and children. This is a difficult time that can bring worries of ill judgment by your peers and community. Remember that it is our deeds which define our character. Focus on your daily actions that reflect the person you really are. When you recover control of your identity again you'll be a stronger and better person.

Often, many years after separation, the mother of your children continues to find ways in which to play on your sense of duty. She makes use of guilt and shame to get you to do simple things such as always being the one who drops off and picks up the children, to more complex tasks like procuring your child's placement at a school of her choosing. "Be a good father" is the usual stated reason.

Aggression or bullying can take many forms, not all of which are easily identifiable. Women employ passive aggressive methods to pretend fairness while manipulating subtle emotional weaknesses by interjecting children into the scenario. One example is where the mother will tell you that she tried to talk the kids out of a summer day camp that prevents you from having time with them but they were too excited and she didn't want to disappoint them. This camp will be something they heard of because she told them about it, and she'll ask you to break the news to them that they can't go. No parent enjoys having to say no to an excited child. The parent initiating the placement of a child into this position is a poor parent.

As Winston Churchill said, "Nothing in life is so exhilarating as to be shot at without result."

CHAPTER 5:   THERAPY IMPROVES YOUR ODDS

*That the birds of worry and care fly above
your head this you cannot change. But
that they build nests in your hair you can
prevent.*

— Chinese proverb

Most men are too caught up being stoic or angry to fully appreciate the draining toll their family break-up is taking on them. Those who do recognize their condition may still believe they can muscle right on through and sooner or later, "I'll be okay." This lack of self-care is even more pronounced in men who have been emotionally abused throughout the relationship and have come to accept their depleted and defeated self as normal. The rate of accidents, illness, and suicide goes up markedly for recently divorced men. Therapy can prevent you from becoming one of those statistics.

As I've said in previous chapters, this book is for men who can't afford the expense of a lawyer and it may seem absurd to suggest spending money on a therapist when you can't even pay for professional legal defense. If you have insurance coverage for therapy through your work, take advantage of it. It's free and it can only improve your case. This is not a secondary issue. When you are standing before a judge they will be assessing your psyche as well as your sincerity. If you want to win, you must enter the arena sound in body and sound in mind. Regardless of how much money you might have spent on a lawyer, it won't help you if you enter the courtroom in a mentally imbalanced state. The judge will be looking for emotional problems. Your ex will be listing them. Don't let the judge find one.

All men going through a divorce benefit from working on their emotional health in whatever way is available. For those who have addictions or anger problems, you must show an awareness and willingness to address those problems head-on if you want good parenting time with your children.

Doctors tell us that there is a discernible grieving process following the death of a loved one or the end of a serious relationship. It normally takes about two years to fully recover just from the "death" of the relationship itself. The agony of a protracted dispute involving children seriously compounds and lengthens an already life shattering experience.

Self-awareness, self-healing, depression, guilt, and anger are things that will respectively impress or negatively influence a judge in your hearing. The judge is there to see what kind of parents you both are. If you can show that you are aware of and engaged in promoting mental and emotional health for you and your children it will work to your benefit. You are not the only person struggling with upheaval and stress, and to help your children cope with this important life change you need to be addressing the mental health and safety of all involved. Taking a proactive approach with counseling does not mean that you are admitting any illness or vulnerability. It will show a judge that you are willing and able to ask for ideas to ensure your family's safety. While not a guarantee of court success, showing awareness and concern for emotional health improves a father's odds in court.

Don't hide that you are seeing a therapist and, if your ex's lawyer tries to paint that as evidence that you are unfit, judges will agree that you are actually showing responsibility in ensuring a stable home. That being said, try to keep your therapy focused on the issues related to proper parenting.

WARNING: Counselor's notes from your sessions can easily be subpoenaed, though the counselor himself is rarely called to testify. Find a therapist who agrees to limit or avoid notes on your sessions. Never forget that your counselor can be compelled by your ex or her/his lawyer to come to court with your file. Unless there is a court order giving your counselor privilege, they can report things you may not want anyone to know, that may be personal childhood issues, or things that could be used against you. Most women's shelters and many women's counselors don't take or keep notes for that exact reason. Stick to the issues that relate to balancing your emotions about the divorce and how to bring stability back to your children's lives. Save your personal childhood issues for another time in your life.

The One School of Thought

When looking at different forms of therapy, be aware that there are many different styles. Counselors have different schools of thought and employ different methods of discovery. Some will work better for you than others. Whether you can afford a therapist or do your own independent self-healing work, try to find one approach that fits with you then focus on doing it well.

In practical terms, let's say that you want to learn how to ski. Suppose there are four different schools of thought or training as to how best to learn to ski. You can investigate each school, interview each of the four instructors all you want, but sooner or later you have to flip a coin and pick one. Each has all the components to go from beginner to medium to good. You shouldn't pick and choose tips and suggestions from each or you may end up with skis tied around the trunk of a tree. Once you learn the basics of one school, then, and only then, is your mind and body ready to experiment with the other styles.

Before you can benefit from the many you need to be rooted in one.

CHAPTER 6: UNDERSTANDING ANXIETY

"When the world is storm driven and the
bad that happens and the worse that
threatens are so urgent as to shut out
everything else from view, then we need to
know all the strong fortresses of the spirit
which men have built through the ages."

– Edith Hamilton, The Greek Way

Anxiety is a constant companion in the lives of fathers struggling through separation. At some level it is always there. Not knowing what new accusation or legal assault is around the next corner in a letter from her lawyer or a call from the police, fearing some freshly invented allegations against you more outrageous than the last.

It's not just your income, your access to your children, and the loss of your home that you are facing, but your very identity is under a magnifying glass and someone you've never met, a judge, is going to decide whether or not he/she believes you when you say who you are as a person. Your ex and her mouth-for-hire lawyer will be painting lurid tales, crafting her story out of embarrassing moments, normally hidden from the world, and quite often fabricating evidence against you from whole cloth. This is a battle with no winners.

If your time with your children is limited right now you may be afraid that the slightest conflict or attempt to discipline them will be spun into a toxic tale of abuse. Many fathers will be struggling with increased financial load, having to pay support and having two homes to pay for. If your ex is in the family home, your new location has to compete with the comfort of the one they've grown up in.

You want your home to be comfortable for them and to fill it with new toys, clothes that can be kept there, access to entertainment, and have them feel attachment to this secondary new home you have to offer. Even if you have the resources to create a second home they are excited to visit, their friends may not be as accessible to them when they visit.

You have many questions and worries circling your mind. How much money is a judge going to make you pay your wife? Will you be able to afford it? Will your once common friends believe all the lies she is now telling them? Can you keep your cool and not say or do something you may regret? Will your kids start to see you as their mother does? How do you answer their honest questions and comfort them without involving them in the fight? How do you hide your anxiety from your children so they aren't frightened?

This is a time of natural anxiety and, when you are feeling weak, remember that your anxiety makes sense. It is not an unknown beast. Acknowledge your stress and that it is connected to an event that will eventually pass.

Anxiety and stress are recognized as major contributors to poor mental and physical health. You need to address these conditions right away. If you are experiencing a high degree of anxiety that is interfering with your ability to perform daily tasks you should consider getting some relief from anti-anxiety medication after a conversation with your doctor. Don't feel too proud or worry what others might think if your doctor thinks this would be a good solution for you.

Meditative practices are good antidotes to stress and for some just creating new routines or habits that are healthy can be a form of mindfulness. Your life has an emptiness right now and you may try to fill it with addictions to alcohol, work, or sex. Moderation is the key. You need to be there for your children and the best way to do that is to be there for yourself. Don't fight your mind, learn to understand it. When your mind strays to places that aren't helpful then learn to guide yourself back to a state that is balanced.

Self-help books stores are well stocked with reputable authors giving advice on stress, anxiety, and depression. Flip through the pages and sample sections from throughout the whole book to see if the author's voice resonates with you before buying it. Take the parts that work for you and just leave behind the things that don't feel right.

When faced with worry remember this: If there is something you can do about what bothers you, do it. If there isn't, then let it go. There is no point obsessing over things that can't be changed at that moment. Try to focus on the areas of your life which you can affect. You can't change other people; you can only change yourself and how you react to others. This simple truth, like all simple truths, is easy to say and damned hard to live by. With practice you can learn to categorize your worries and keep focused on the things you can change. To worry is to pay negative energy interest on trouble before it even appears. Remember that lies are always flawed and, if your ex is misrepresenting the truth, the best chance you have to expose it is to be focused and calm.

Because anxiety can have such deleterious effects on your mental state and your health, it is absolutely critical you maintain a consistent schedule of being checked out by a trusted doctor throughout your ordeal. If you share a doctor with your ex, assess your confidence in his or her ability to maintain your privacy. If necessary, find a new doctor that you can trust. If your doctor recommends anxiety medication, ask questions about the various options and have an honest discussion about your concerns and how this might help you.

A bad antidote to relieve negative energy and stress is to retreat into victim status. Telling yourself others are responsible for your problems lifts the cloud of self-blame.

Victimhood is viewing the world, and those in it, as unfairly dealing with you, out to get you, and yourself merely a passive player. Focusing on the negative brings about a sense of powerlessness wherein someone or something is causing all your problems and others should come to your rescue. In adopting this victimhood stance, you are wrongly taking the position that you are not the least bit personally responsible for your predicament. Seeing yourself as the victim is wrapping heavy chains around your ankles, preventing you from moving forward. Playing the role of victim is not a monopoly, or even the natural terrain, of men. Too many mothers, during the fallout of a broken relationship, are encouraged to adopt the status of victim. For women, victimhood is almost celebrated, under the guise of empowerment. Woman's "historical oppression" becomes her champion in a courtroom whether or not the particular woman you face in court has ever struggled over anything worse than a broken fingernail. Faced with unresolved childhood issues, women often blame their husbands – and often all men – for their troubled place in life. Victims seek to fix the blame and not the problem. The same trick will not work for you and will only make your situation worse.

Stress, fear, and anxiety can be reduced by learning to re-frame your world. As the Greek philosopher, Epictetus, said, "It is not things in themselves that trouble us, but our opinions of things."

Marcus Aurelius, wrote in Meditations, "If you are distressed by anything external, the pain is not due to the thing itself, but to your estimate of it; and this you have the power to revoke at any moment." He held that we are not hurt by the acts others do against us, it is our own views and beliefs about those bad acts that do the harm.

Perhaps no philosopher, religious preacher or psychologist has put it more directly than Shakespeare in Hamlet when he says "There is nothing either good or bad, but thinking makes it so."

Encapsulated in this one short statement, of Hamlet to Rosencrantz, is all the inherited wisdom of mankind needed to live a happy, compassionate, and fruitful life. It is terribly difficult for most people to grasp this profound truth. Very few ever persist in its pursuit. You must adopt this truth as your walking stick.

Your peace of mind improves in direct proportion to your ability to push your pause button between being acted upon by an external event or stimulus and permitting yourself to respond unconsciously without proper perspective. The middle road can best be found by training your mind to understand that it is your own perceptions, biases, and expectations that cause you to feel and act the way you do. You always have a choice. When you understand that, your anxiety will start to fade.

Rarely can one say that there is a single practice that can help any and every person who tries it. That can be said about mindfulness and meditation. If all you do after reading this book is take up mindfulness and meditation, you will be amazed at the result.

CHAPTER 7:   UNTYING THE KNOTS OF ANGER

There was a very powerful ethic in older cultures that taught men to seek revenge on those who did them wrong or wronged others. An eye for an eye! Men were made to feel weak and of poor character if they weren't on guard to right such wrongs. Even today, when a woman feels wronged she will often turn to a man to be her champion.

The very behavior demanded of men, this "fight back" response, is now his condemnation. Violence in the world is now almost strictly referred to as "male violence." Accusations of violence increasingly accompany requests for divorce in order to gain the most favorable conditions for the mother. An angry response will only feed the fuel for her lies. Despite this danger, fathers must subdue their mythical inner avenger. Signs of anger will work against you in the courtroom

Badly hurt by the mother of their children, fearing the loss of their relationship with them, some men have trouble overcoming the rawness of their rage. Anger is natural, especially where lies are being told, your reputation may be in jeopardy, and you might have been forced to spend some nights in jail on false accusations. These are tough pills to swallow. What you don't want, and what your children don't need, is for you to become the very thing you are trying to prove is untrue. By activating this anger in you, she might well turn you into the villain she wants everyone to see.

When it comes to the loss of a relationship with the mother of your child, seeking any kind of revenge is absolutely the worst thing you can do. It will cause you to lose badly in any court proceedings and, worst of all, it will poison the relationship with your ex to the extent that neither one of you will be able to parent your children as well as you otherwise might. This does not mean you should suppress or deny your anger. Not at all. What you need is control, and a productive way to deal with your natural emotions. Vent your anger in non-destructive ways.

To survive the loss of your relationship and create a new, more dynamic relationship with your children, you must give up visions of revenge, cast off the cloak of victimhood, and find the middle path.

I had one client who was particularly stuck in victim-anger. The wrongs done to him and his children by his former wife were outrageous. His life had been made miserable. It became apparent to me that this man could not move forward, up, and onward into his life. Instead, he remained mired in his need for revenge. He saw the court as a forum where some fundamental truth of his life would come out, where he would finally be vindicated in all things, and his wife condemned and excommunicated. I spent over a year trying to release him from his own past, but to no avail. Over lunch in the middle of trial I commented to him, in my ever-pressing message to escape his past, that it was true that fate had dealt him a very bad hand. I will never forget his immediate response: "Why me? Why has fate done this to me?"

I leaped on that comment. I tried again to drive home my belief that the trial to protect his children's rights was not the time to answer that question. I told him after the trial he would have the rest of his life to try and figure that out. I told him what the Stoics would have told him: Accept the changes in your life, no matter how they have been arrived at. Get on with it. The past cannot be undone. Do the very best you can. You really have no choice. Being a good father, for its own sake, does not require your ex to see it or agree.

I told him that the "why me" victim question is very normal at first. Ask the question. Realize there really is no satisfactory answer and then drop it. There never is a right answer to "Why me?" It just is. Get on with dealing with it. How you move forward is the most important question to answer right now.

I give this very same message to all my clients, fathers, and mothers. Nearly all can be made to understand and accept it eventually. It is a time-consuming exercise. Continuing to ask the "Why Me?" question is the wrong question. Only when I can convince my client to focus on the future for a sufficiently long enough period of time does the "Why Me?" syndrome fade away.

Anger possesses no independent existence. Anger, for most people, is a momentary state in an otherwise non-angry person. It arises because of certain conditions, and it goes away when replaced by a subsequent set of improved conditions. The narrative your ex is trying to create is that your anger is deep seated and irrational. She will claim this anger is ever present inside of you and she doesn't know what brings it out, all the while pressing those buttons she's learned so well to trigger anger. That is why you need to deactivate those buttons.

Most anger is destructive. We get angry at ourselves and keep it suppressed, not expressing it in a healthy way. We get angry outwardly at other people or things. If we confuse frustration with anger it can lead to rage, causing injury to others and, ultimately, to ourselves.

The frustration a father feels when he suddenly can't see his children as much as he used to is universal and very understandable. Every caring and nurturing parent experiences that frustration, sense of loss, and grief. Those emotions usually trigger anger at the mother of the children, at oneself, and at the "system" which is biased in favor of mothers.

Some men are unable to control that anger and end up making things worse for themselves and their children. Others, fearful of what they might do or say, retreat from the whole scene and essentially abandon their kids. Most get motivated by the anger to change their circumstance. The degree to which fathers actually are successful in meaningfully changing their circumstances is inversely proportional to the degree that they let their anger continue to motivate them. High anger brings low results. Controlled, understood, and reduced anger brings about better and more lasting changes in one's circumstance.

The adage "Don't get angry – get even!" is only half right. Getting "even" still has too much of a connotation of anger in it. A better one is: "Don't get angry – get focused!" The more you get to know yourself, the better able you will be to understand how and why external circumstances trigger negative emotions. Only by such understanding do you have any chance of turning it into positive energy. That energy is required to fuel improvements to your current predicament.

The trick is to be able to take control of and responsibility for the way you feel. You feel the way you do, with any emotion be it good or bad, because of the way you perceive it, interpret it, or let it affect you. This can be a conscious or unconscious reaction.

You will gain a subtler and more interesting awareness when you learn to recognize your feeling of being trapped, a slave to what others do and say, as a knee-jerk emotional reaction. You must move from letting your emotions govern you when it should be you in control of your emotions. Recognize that you have been surviving on behavioral strategies designed to avoid the pain of your true reality. That explosive awareness motivates a tenacious desire to bust out of that cage and start actively living again.

> "Anger plays an important role when
> there is a bad blow to the ego. It
> temporarily shields the betrayed from
> facing devastating emotions: grief,
> rejection, even self-hatred." – Constance
> Ahrons, Ph.D., The Good Divorce.

The key word in Dr. Ahrons' statement is "temporarily." It is never too soon to start understanding and dealing with the anger.

I appreciate how easy it is for me to preach this sermon of salvation to men I have never met. Men whose life experiences are unique to themselves, whose despair, pain, fear, and personal experience of hell heading to divorce court want a lawyer to give them survival skills, not personal advice. What I hope you realize by now is that no one entirely wins in a nasty divorce. Oscar Wilde said he only lost two lawsuits: once when he lost and once when he won.

Make a list of all the things that trigger your anger. Examine the list to discern the primary issues. It is important to dedicate a great deal of time and energy to understanding and neutralizing these knots of negative energy. Otherwise, they will continue to dictate and determine your behaviour. Some of the anger triggers may have been formed many years ago, and will require more serious work to break up. Others may be more recent. Start with the easier ones first. The more control you have over your anger and the physical signs of anger, the more successful you'll be when asking a judge to trust you.

Psychologists like to tell us to "vent" our anger. Don't keep it bottled up. Take a baseball bat and hit a big oak tree. This psychology is best optimized by the scene in the movie *Analyze This* (1999) when the psychiatrist played by Billy Crystal is telling the panic-attack stricken mob boss played by Robert De Niro that, to relieve his frustration he should "hit something." The patient thinks for a moment, pulls out his pistol, aims into a nearby chair and fires several rounds into a quickly decimated pillow. The slightly stunned psychiatrist says, "There, you feel better?" To which the mob boss responds: "Yeah, I do."

Venting anger might feel good at the time, but it provides only temporary relief. You have to get to the root.

It is your ego that gets angry. Someone or something has offended or challenged it. What expectations are being challenged? Having shed your former self-concept like a snake skin, your strengthened sense of self should not be as easily offended. Once you have accomplished this, it will be more difficult for your attackers to succeed in painting you as a villain or a menace in the courtroom. Your self-control and awareness will be your strength when the judge is assessing credibility.

Over time, people will see through the lies of others if you remain consistent in your actions.

Anger shows itself when one or more triggers are set off. Familiarize yourself with all the triggers which set off your negative feelings that can lead to an act of anger. Practice learning to recognize an angry act as comprising 3 separate components.

The obvious one is the angry act itself. A second is the emotional sea of negative emotions that fuel the angry act. These emotions arise from the third stage which is where the brain interprets stimuli coming from the external environment or memory. The third stage is the collectivity of emotional and body sensations that are interpreted by your ego as negative that becomes the trigger for the act of anger

The 3 stages actually occur in reverse order. First is the reception by your senses of external stimuli or internal memories. Your brain and hormone systems interpret those stimuli as they have been trained by you to do. Here is the first and best place to change your behavior in terms of how your ego chooses to interpret the stimuli. It is up to you. This is where your mind is about to decide to interpret the stimuli as either negative, neutral or positive. With practice you can train your brain to give you a heads up when it is about to make the important choice. From memory and experience, you will immediately know if the brain is about to interpret the stimuli as negative. Jump in and take back control. Turn the stimuli neutral, or even better, positive. But at the very least close the door on it coming out negative. This stage is the most difficult to achieve.

The second stage is when the brain and the hormones communicate to all the cells that the stimuli should be interpreted as negative. That message comes in the form of angry emotions. The trick here of course is to not let the anger vent in a negative way, against someone or yourself. Don't keep it bottled up. Get it out by talking to a buddy, taking a long run, hit the tree out back with a bat. Don't drink or toke up.

If that fails, you are in stage 3 and have released your destructive emotions. You swear or hit something. It is too late to stop it, but not too late to learn how to prevent it from happening again. Go back to stage 2 and practice, practice, practice.

The more you practice stage 2 the more focus you will find you have on stage 1.

An example of a neutral stimuli having two different interactions. You are standing on the edge of the Grand Canyon. You yell out your name: "Paul is a stupid son of a bitch!" An echo bounces back from the opposite wall of the canyon: "Paul is a stupid son of a bitch!" "Wow," you say to yourself. "How cool is that?" You receive the words in the echo with warmth and humor. But minutes later, out of nowhere, from a different direction, from a different voice, you hear: "Paul is a stupid son of a bitch!"

Before your untrained mind can intervene, your injured ego triggers a strong negative emotion. You are jolted.

Why? The exact same words. The same meaning. The first makes you chuckle. The 2nd sets off hormones, increased blood pressure, and defense mechanism around your ego.

There are dozens of self-help books on how to control anger. Anger management classes are full of referrals from a variety of agencies. Their common purpose is to help you control an assumed anger problem. A rare few attempt to teach you how not to become upset in the first place. I recommend you read "*Destructive Emotions: How Can We Overcome Them? A Scientific Dialogue with the Dalai Lama*" by Daniel   Goleman.

CHAPTER 8: DEPRESSION – SILENT SABOTAGE

Depression can creep up on you or body slam you on a concrete floor. It is a natural response to negative events. Left without attention, depression can cause you to become dysfunctional. For some, depression is not a temporary state but an ongoing clinical problem they may not even know has been lurking under the surface of their daily lives until something pushes the problem into a spotlight.

Though taboos around depression are being lifted through the hard work of mental illness awareness groups, there is still a stigma attached to depression. People think you're just being lazy, or a pessimist, or giving into weakness, unless they've experienced it themselves. Depression can manifest as annoyance at simple things or can be as obvious as having difficulty getting out of bed.

Going through a divorce is a reasonable cause for situational depression. It is a condition that must be monitored and checked. Failing to do so could be a huge mistake. Friends or family who are concerned about you are a good source of feedback. Don't regard signs of depression as a temporary problem which will soon end if you just ignore it. It won't! According to Statistics Canada (2007), men are twice as likely to suffer depression than women after a divorce.

Rather than face up to the serious reality of their condition, men too frequently resort to increased external stimulus for relief. The typical ones which work best in the short term are lots of exercise, making more money, and sex. Male stereotypes convince depressed men that they can just muscle through the pain, uncomplaining, and it will all eventually get better. Don't take that chance. If depression is causing problems, you must seek the advice of a doctor. Many people don't have a regular doctor and just go to walk in clinics. This will not be useful when you're dealing with a problem that requires repeat visits with a doctor who knows your situation and something about your history.

The urge to self-medicate adds another dimension of dysfunction for men who turn to alcohol and drugs to mask their despair. While it might give you temporary relief, it will not bring you closer to your children. What you need right now is a sense of control over your future.

Depression is part of the normal grieving process in the loss of a relationship. Like the death of a loved one, an event that eventually affects us all, a divorce means you will no longer be able to do all the things you might have dreamed with the people you've bonded with and built your life around. No matter how well you do in court, you will never get back the life you dreamed of creating for your children. You might be able to create something new, but you cannot repair what was lost. Additionally, you may experience a loss of, or suspicion from, former friends, difficulties at work, and minor health problems from this stressful time in your life. To deal with these losses in a productive way you need to attend to your mental health and make sure that natural depression doesn't interfere with your goals as a parent.

At a time when you need to be able to call on all your inner strengths, depression can work in a very sinister way to defeat those strengths and to undercut your will. It may be a seductive voice that sits on the shoulder of your mind and tells you that nothing is worth doing. Why bother? She has the courts on her side. Her lawyer is unethical. Have another drink. Your brain tells your endocrine system to pump more mood-suppressing chemicals into your blood to really tie you down in despair. Soon you may find yourself seriously entertaining previously foreign thoughts such as "what's the use," or "it would be easier all around if I just gave up and let her have the kids." Your self-esteem is replaced by shame, defeated will power, and a deadening sense of hopelessness.

If you feel defeated before your divorce is completed, go see your doctor. Tell them a lawyer sent you. Ask for an assessment and be willing to consider the options available to bring you relief while you struggle with the divorce. If you decide to take medication, also be aware of the side effects and what to expect while you adapt to the prescription. Anti-depressants do not work the same for everyone and it may take some time to find the right course of treatment. If you are experiencing dysfunctional depression, medication can give you some temporary relief and you should consider it seriously. Just as seriously, if you decide to take medication, make sure you are working with a doctor you trust and that you have a road map for your treatment.

Proper medical care with the right drugs can work wonders.

Depression breeds victimhood. If you allow yourself to be the victim in your personal narrative, then who is going to be there for your children? They are the real victims in a divorce, and they need you.

Beyond what the technical description of depression is and how doctors diagnose it, your main concern is to unload the baggage of your past and focus on creating a stable future. People often enter into relationships carrying depressive baggage and being unaware of it, or, if aware, failing to deal with it, allow it to eat away at the relationship. Women are just as guilty of this as men are. Betty Friedan's "Problem With No Name" was essentially about housewives suffering from malaise who often ended up on medication for depression. Instead of dealing with their lack of participation in life, they chose to blame men for their problems. This socially motivated investigation has yet to move over to a similar look at male depression where it is seen as unmanly. For men, it is commonly thought that your career and your income potential is what brings you satisfaction and the only cure needed for your woes is to learn how to make more money. For men, the concern that they are not fulfilled by their emotional life, or the loss of their childhood dreams, is suppressed and considered selfish so their depression can appear as a silent anger simmering under the surface.

Now that you are getting divorced, you can divorce yourself from the lack of self-care that was formerly just part of your "job" as a man. When you care about your own happiness you can bring more joy to your children's lives.

Role Breakdown

The break down in the traditional roles of men and women in all aspects of life are difficult for many men to adjust to. Workplaces have changed, eliminating job security and confidence in being a stable provider. Marriage, for many, offers the lure of combining energy, if not resources, to accomplish stability. Divorce is a nuclear bomb in this illusion. For men, divorce means a loss of your "team" and doubles the demands on your resources. While feminists, through the ever expanding avenues of social media and indoctrination into institutions of higher learning, have been preaching that women are further from equality than ever, men facing divorce know better. These zealots, while claiming oppression, demand superiority over the presumed oppressive male when it comes to claiming rights and privileges, but with none of the obligations. The hysterical claims by the radical victim feminists over the past decades that all men are rapists and the cause of every evil in society can nag subtly at the conscience of good men confused by all the changes in post-modern society.

It's enough to make a man depressed.

Men in divorce have an ex-partner spewing out the rhetoric of oppression while having the ability to obtain court orders against you based on violence that never happened and imaginary emotional states.

Some men can be too easily controlled and motivated by this shaming. These particular mothers do this by cloaking themselves in gender morality. None of these factors get much attention in the mainstream of psychology. Toss all of these contagious ingredients into a father's psychological blender and you get a dark toxic drink. The coup de grâce is that the ignorance of lawyers, judges, and the psychological experts who advise the courts, serves only to further enable these mothers. Men caught in this trap commit suicide four times more often than women. The cover-up continues.

The subject of depression is too large and important to do any justice with here. Even if you don't think you are suffering from depression, recognize that you are the worst judge of that. Go see your doctor. In addition, I strongly recommend you consider picking up a copy of the book "I Don't Want to Talk About It" by Terrence Real, which deals with the topic expertly. I've seen clients who never knew the degree to which they were depressed eventually come out of it amazed at the freshness and clarity of their new life. It is the experience of a person, near sighted their whole life, suddenly putting on a pair of good glasses. A new world unfolds.

Sometimes it's not you that is crazy, it's the world around you. My advice is to make sure you know which is which and to take care of yourself so that you can be a good father to your children. Children who spend time with depressed parents suffer and may even take on the symptoms. While you struggle with all the important and real issues that you are facing, make sure your children are spared the same ordeal.

Again, I can't commend mindfulness meditation enough to help with depression.

Psychedelic Psychotherapy

I am writing this chapter in the fall of 2016. In Europe and North America there is a scientific/psychological renaissance underway. The breakthrough experiments and studies of the 1950's and 1960's with psychedelics and mental illness, alcoholism, addictions and aberrant behavior that were outlawed in the 1970's, are once again getting support from government and the health professions. The legalization of cannabis for medical purposes is only the most popular and obvious of these progressive developments. Cannabis and MDMA and psychedelics are demonstrating dramatic results helping a wide variety of illnesses. When administered by a trained therapist or psychiatrist, in the proper set and setting, depression is one of those illnesses helped.

You could do your own research on this subject. You might find help.

CHAPTER 9:   HIT THE GYM

There is a lot more value to getting physically fit than just revenge, but if that's what you need to get you motivated then go for it. A divorce is demoralizing. Make working on the "better you" your new lifestyle and you'll find many benefits from physical fitness.

Developing a good fitness routine can work like meditation. You don't need to look like Adonis or Atlas or, god forbid, Arnold Schwarzenegger (The Governator), but getting fit will improve your ability to handle stress both mentally and physically.

Don't commit yourself to a year-long membership right away, which I understand is notoriously hard to cancel. Start by assessing your physical fitness and thinking about where your weaknesses are then go on the internet to look up how to improve this part of your body or health. You can design relatively cheap fitness programs for yourself if you do your research well. You can incorporate fitness into your time with your kids by planning hiking trips. Children need fitness too and you can educate them about nature while you're on the hike.

Men with health routines have pride in their fitness. If that's your case, continuing these habits can provide a meditation space where you can let your frustrating thoughts emerge so they can dissipate. Be careful not to harm yourself by letting anger cause you to push yourself too hard in whatever routine you design. You'll find if you let angry thoughts express themselves while you are working out, walking, or jogging, and you don't focus on them but just observe them and let them go, it will release your mind as well as your body. You might find yourself ranting in an imaginary argument with your ex while you exercise. Find a point where you feel you've said what needed to be said and then laugh at how well things go when you're only fighting with yourself.

If we could play both ourselves and our adversaries the script would always turn out well. When you are jogging or working out at the gym you should always make the better argument. By the end of the session, not only will you know you are "right," you'll be a bit healthier. But remember arguments in court are not so easily controlled. The more times you let these frustrating conversations play out in your head the better practiced you'll be in making your case to a judge. And you'll look good doing it.

Plan activities for your kids that are actually active and keep a log of what you do when they visit. Not only will this show a commitment to the wellbeing of your children, they'll have fun and you will be including them in your new lifestyle. Don't over plan their visits though. Kids like to have down time and play video games and if you try to pack your time with a full agenda it will be overwhelming and unnatural. Even if you start these trips out thinking "I bet they're having more fun with me than with their mom!" what you are striving for is not a competition but a real engagement with your children so the time you spend together is more meaningful.

This is the start of your new life. Make it happy, healthy, and rewarding.

Our culture is obsessed with beauty and physical attractiveness. The Greeks are just one of many cultures who valued and championed the ideal of perfection of the body as well as the mind. You don't have to be a Greek sculpture. Just focus on being a healthy version of the former you. For men facing a difficult divorce, most have endured sexual and physical rejection for a lengthy time leading up to the separation. Getting back in touch with your physical self is an import step in gaining the confidence you need in court. As you become more satisfied with yourself you'll find yourself feeling less angry with your ex. The harm she has done to your esteem will fade away and you'll be less vulnerable when she says disparaging things about you in the courtroom.

To a large extent, our society has given up on seeing our bodies as a basic part of ourselves needing the kind of attention we now reserve only for our egos and career ambitions. The ideal of a healthy body lives on in the West only symbolically and is paid little more than lip service except during the Olympic Games. Even our grade schools have had their physical education programs gutted or complicated by concerns over "fat shaming" or various other oppression claims that can make schools vulnerable to lawsuits. Healthy competition has been replaced with community service requirements and energetic kids might find themselves put on drugs like Ritalin.

For men, part of getting through a divorce is rediscovering and coming back into contact with your physical body and learning how to honor it. A man estranged from his body is estranged from nature. Body and mind are one. Each directly impacts the other. The point is to practice self-care. Your children will learn by example. Also, your ex may want you to get fat and depressed. Don't let her win.

CHAPTER 10: THE BLAME GAME

"Nothing is more wretched than the
mind of a man conscious of guilt." –
Plautus, c. 254 – 184 BC

I t is very common for one or both separating partners to be overcome with a deep and unshakable sense of guilt. In a manner, difficult to articulate, failed relationships often create an urge to find a source of blame in order to make sense of the events. Fathers blame themselves for the failure, not just for the marriage, but of the dream of the hero they were going to be for their children. But that dream was still-born in the first place, a naïve projection by our culture onto every young man. The blame, if there is to be any, should be on the institutions of society which seduce us into thinking that there is actually reality in the materialistic values sold to us in the marketplace. So don't accept any guilt for waking up to your own actual and very personal reality. Consider yourself lucky.

The emotion of guilt is a strong drag on getting beyond your past and into your future. Guilt serves no purpose but to prevent us from clearly seeing and understanding our own actions and thoughts forward. We must minimize the impact of guilt upon our mind and appreciate more the sense of regret, which implies understanding and cognition. It is, therefore, important to fully face and concentrate on coming to terms with this emotion.

High negative judgment on yourself or others when relationships don't work out is unfair to you and to your former partner. People, though inherently decent, can act in irregular ways because of stress or conflict. You were – and perhaps remain – caught up in circumstances not entirely of your own making. None of us are solely responsible for the circumstances of our early lives. None of us are responsible for what our parents and childhood failed to provide us with or protect us from. And to a great extent, neither are our parents. It's the human condition.

To diminish guilt, you must take full acceptance of the events you feel guilty about, accept them as just part of life – shit happens – and get on with things. Substitute the emotion of guilt with the more rational and reasoning concept of examined regret. Any real ability to fully understand yourself and your life is blocked by the emotionally driven desire to condemn, whether it be condemnation of yourself with guilt or your ex with blame. To regret is not to condemn. When the sensation of guilt arises next – as it will for a while – just welcome it. Use its reappearance in your heart and mind to trigger your focus back to a mindful attention to regret instead. Reflect on what you have learned from the experience, and soon guilt will come less frequently and eventually be gone. Eventually you take the same approach to reasoning away regret as well. Regret is based on living in the past, wishing things were different, and your goal is start focusing on the opportunities held by the future.

At a deeper level there is a connection between feeling guilty – blaming yourself – and blaming your former partner. Both are understandable and universal knee jerk emotional reactions to the collapse of your world. But we know that neither blaming yourself or blaming your ex serves a useful purpose. Not only will it not help you in any meaningful way, it will serve as a major force to keep you mired in the mud of your past.

At its most fundamental level, "blame" arises from our habit to judge everything. We judge ourselves, we judge others. We live in a world of comparisons. It is our compulsive act of judging everything and everybody which ultimately needs to be understood and controlled. Judging less permits our negative attitudes, thoughts and emotions to calm and lesson. While it is admittedly going to be damned near impossible at this point in your life not to want to judge – you might be standing in front of one soon – it is nevertheless true that you must make every effort to be open and understanding. Important and tangible results flow when you are less judgmental. You feel better – a lot better! You will be a better role model to your children. Just as importantly, a judge in a courtroom will find you a far more credible parent and witness when you arrive seeking solutions instead of blame. In other words, the less you judge, the better you will be judged.

You would be surprised at how few aspects of our lives we must have an opinion on, or judge. Practice regarding what your senses make you aware of as being totally neutral, neither good nor bad.

If you create and cling to justifications which argue that you were right and she was wrong, you will be forcing that binary thinking into the hands of the court. Not judging is part of the goal of not needing to win but, instead, seeking just outcomes. If you are struggling with guilt, shame, or a need to blame your ex, that is the first judgment you have to pass.

There is another important reason to remove the very real emotion of guilt from inside your head: shame can be the strongest weapon your ex is able to use against you and may be something she has been employing for many years. She knows all the right buttons to push. Feelings that you aren't good enough, that you failed, that you were the source of all the problems, are the lifeblood of her control. If you respond to these feelings with aggression you will also be playing into her hands. As long as you hold guilt in your mind, your ex has a large target to aim at. With your guilt gone that target vanishes.

The shaming tactics to watch for mostly look the same. Ad hominem attacks, or attempts to attack your character with labels such as "woman hater," "misogynist," "angry drunk," or "narcissist," are meant to put you on the defensive and draw out anger that will bolster their claims. If you find yourself under attack, absorb the blows. Remind everyone it's sad your ex would say such nasty things about the father of her children.

CHAPTER 11: FORTRESS OF HOPE

*"If one does not know to which port one
is sailing, no wind is favorable."*

— Seneca

A rmies can lose battles but still win the war. Boxers can lose every round but still score a knock out at the end of the fight. You must be prepared to suffer setbacks. As long as you don't give up on your children, you can still win in the end. For many, the "end" will be a trial. Or on the court house steps before the trial. Then it is a new beginning. If this is where you are headed, it is important to have your own thought out definition of success or winning. For a middle weight to be able to go 10 rounds with a heavy weight and not get knocked down would be a great success. To lose only 20% in a stock market crash where the average loss is 40% is a success. In a gender-biased court, to get three days and nights a week with your children is a success. Nevertheless, you'll never get what you don't ask for. Craft your goals realistically but with hope.

Robert Browning says that a man's reach should exceed his grasp. When determining what it is that you want for your children, when you frame your court application, it is critical that you pay little attention to those voices who say you "must be reasonable", that you should lower your expectations. Utter nonsense! Free yourself from what you have read. Follow your heart and ask for what you truly feel is best for your children. Now is not the time to compromise with their future.

If you get advice from a lawyer, ignore those who say they have merely "represented" or "appeared" for a father. Anyone fresh out of law school can do that. You want someone who has "fought" for a father. Only consider that person's advice and weigh it against your goals.

A prerequisite is to recognize just how much of your thinking process and ambition has been stunted by the emotional abuse suffered at the hands of the mother. Don't define the possible in terms dictated by the mother. Don't believe the words "Oh no, she would never agree to that." Job one is to free your imagination and spirit from the years of crippling control by the mother of your children. Emotional abuse can be a very subtle but deep wound.

Challenge yourself to discover where your confidence fails and ask yourself if it is based in reality or if it comes from negativity that you have been subjected to over time. Your hope for a better future will show when you present your case in court. The more you believe in yourself, the more a judge will believe in the positive environment you have to offer your children. Hope for the best and steel yourself for disappointments along the way.

Hope is a very interesting and important sentiment. It signifies usually that there is something unacceptable about the present that "hopefully" will improve in the future. For those unable to accept and live fully and totally in the present – most of us – it provides a reason to keep going forward. It softens the hard edges of the moment. It is our vision of what is to become. This is very important for most people. On the other hand, hope can deceive us into thinking that we don't have to learn to live in the present, to accept who and what we are right now. Hope can also make it easier to deal with, or ignore, concerns of the moment because a "better world" lies in the future. This is where hope is a tricky sentiment. In this sense, too much hope can be regarded as a cop out, an excuse to not come to terms with the moment or deal with real problems, but it gives you a target for which to aim.

To have hope is a good thing when it serves to focus on a goal, to believe that our efforts will produce results. The problem occurs when you put too much hope in your hope. If you become so attached to a singular vision that you experience anger or disappointment if something gets in your way, then you need to remember that hope is just a guidepost vision and what you've imagined is not the only good result. Hope is a problem if it causes you to avoid dealing effectively with the here and now in favor a waiting for the object of your hope to materialize at some distant time without the ability to make adjustments.

For men experiencing the loss of their relationship with the mother of their children and a reduction in the relationship between themselves and their children, hope is often all that there is. It is the only emotional life line you can grab onto. My hope in writing this book is that it will help such men to learn to regain reliance upon themselves, family, and friends, in the here and now. A hope to help them find their inner value and truth. Insecurity is not a weakness, it's something we all experience, and when you find yourself struggling to maintain hope your support network can help you find the flexibility to keep you focused.

You can find inspiration from others, from literature, from poets, or from the greatest poet of all – nature. This inspiration is all around you and it's a big part of what you have to offer your children.

Vaclav Havel, a poet and politician, said:

> *"Hope is a dimension of the soul, an orientation of the spirit, an orientation of the heart. It transcends the world that is immediately experienced and is anchored somewhere beyond its horizon. It is not the conviction that something will turn out well, but the certainty that something makes sense regardless of how it turns out."*

No father facing a divorce has any real way of knowing how things are going to turn out. This very feeling of unknowing (at its worst a dark sense of hopelessness, psychological depression, personal worthlessness and despair) is just one more major source of stress in his already chaotic life. Original doubt about the wisdom of leaving the relationship should soon change to confidence in the knowledge that it was the right thing to do. In the short run, it is always hard on the children. How long or short the child suffers depends on how the parents deal with the transition. Your main role is to take your attention away from worry about the future, despair over the past, or anxiety over what sought after changes or results will materialize. Focus primarily on the here and now for your child. Figure out what makes sense for you and sense for your child. Gain insight into yourself, and then find the moral strength to endure, no matter how rough it gets and how little might seem to be gained at the moment.

Thomas Merton, a Catholic Priest, said this about hope:

> *"Do not depend upon the hope of results. You may have to face the fact that your work will be apparently worthless and even achieve no result at all, if not perhaps results opposite to what you expected. As you get used to this idea, you start more and more to concentrate not on the results, but on the value, the rightness, the truth of the work itself. You gradually struggle less and less for an idea and more and more for specific people. In the end, it is the reality of personal relationship that saves everything."*

No good parent needs to be reminded that the most important struggle in their lives is to secure health and happiness for their children. This task is never easy at the best of times and can be particularly difficult during the initial break up. It is during the break up that we come up against the harsh reality that the "dream" you fought for is gone. So it's time to come up with a new dream. A better one.

T.S. Eliot, poet, in 'East Coker', III, Four Quartets :

I said to my soul be still
And wait without hope
For hope would be hope for the wrong thing
And wait without love
For love would be love for the wrong thing
There is yet faith
But the faith and the hope and the love
Are still in the waiting
And do not think
For you are not ready for thought
So the darkness shall be the light
And the stillness the dancing.

Finding yourself in a dark room does not mean there is no light, it just means the light is not currently turned on.

CHAPTER 12:   GET YOUR PRIORITIES STRAIGHT

Ours is a materialistic society and the measure of success is all too often nothing but a test of who can gather up the most physical possessions. Few look upon the man who has found contentment or peace of mind a "success" by our cultural standards. All of us, at some point in our lives, even when our problems are small, remain caught up in the pursuit of material wealth.

It is, therefore, particularly difficult for a father floundering in the wake of a destroyed relationship, fearing for his child's emotional well-being, to have to come to terms with the false god of materialism our society worships. The great minds of the last three millennia have all told us that true understanding and wisdom are acquired when you are in the depths of struggle. If you find yourself focused on the material losses your divorce will bring then it is a sign that you are still stuck in a world where other people determine your value.

It is at this difficult time in your life that you have to come to grips with the nature of desire. Desire for security. Desire to be someone. Desire for things. Desire not to lose things. Desire for the love of your child. Desire for a legacy.

To find the peace, fulfillment, and satisfaction you seek, you must first understand deep in your very being that just as no one can determine who you are, no one can take that identity from you either. When you find yourself focused on what you are losing, remember that you created yourself before and you can create yourself anew. If stripped of your possessions or even the clothes on your back, the source of those things still remains.

Before our minds can calm, and our inner happiness rise to the surface on a full-time basis, we need to let go of the desire for things we don't have. Security, possessions, and emotional fulfillment are always fleeting. We move in cycles and constant change. Success comes when you can adjust to change and maintain your stability. Just as some things come to you only when you stop reaching for them, other things come when you are in the right place to make them happen.

Being a single parent is a new universe. Your life is suddenly upside down and your former dreams, aspirations, and goals are in ruins. As unsympathetic as she may seem right now, your ex is going through a similar upheaval which may be driving some of the behaviors that are frustrating you. Caught in the middle of all this are your children and it's your job to make this time as smooth as possible in terms of their safety and security. The lost dreams are lost for everyone. There are no winners in divorce, least of all the children. What you have in common is confusion, stress, and worry. Primary to both you and your ex is the fear of losing the children. The legal system has adopted an approach that seeks equal access for both parents but the mother is advantaged and she probably knows that.

No mentally healthy rational parent wants to deny their child a meaningful relationship and strong bond with both parents and you need to be rational for the sake of your children. Any parent who acts against this principle is by definition not mentally healthy and will not only raise suspicion in court but will, ultimately, be working against the health of their children.

Efforts to show that your children are the primary concern may help to alleviate problems in the case of some mothers who are operating under a misunderstanding of the father's intentions. Something said or done in the past, or the claims made in court applications that suggest your goal is to exclude her from the child's life may cause her to react as if she's engaged in war. In situations where the mother is not a danger or risk to the children, give her a frank statement of the sharing you seek and put her mind at ease. That may make the process less adversarial.

Do not obsess on what went wrong, why the relationship failed or what you could have done better. The past is the past is the past. People's lives cannot move backwards, only forwards, and the more you allow yourself to ask "what if" questions the less time you have to focus on the future. It doesn't matter if things might have worked out differently had one of you done something differently at a crucial point. They didn't turn out that way so now you have to figure out what to do with the result. Keep yourself looking forward and set a positive example for your kids who are probably more scared and angry than you are right now.

A part of your mind may have convinced you that your ex is now, and will forever remain, your enemy. Keep in mind that this woman is the mother of your child, and she will probably have as much if not more time with your kids than you do. Antagonizing her is not a good idea. Your children will grow up and they will remember how you speak about their mother and will resent being placed in the middle of the battle. Even if your ex is attempting to alienate you, be the better parent and do not use your children as an emotional weapon.

Unless she is sufficiently unfit to be a custodial parent, your ex will remain in the life of your child. Your child will benefit from having two parents who are as mentally healthy as possible. Where there are problems, be aware of the environment you children are experiencing and seek to keep some sort of balance or calm wherever possible. If the mother has mental illness or a personality disorder, by the very nature of her problems she can't recognize it. You will have to make extra effort to overcome the instability and keep things moving forward as productively as possible.

Your ex may not have the kind of physical and psychological stamina and control required to be as good a single parent as she would like to be or as she thought she could be. The less adversarial you are the more likely she will trust you to have the children more often so she can have a night off to pamper herself or have a night out with friends. This can only improve your case. Maybe she just sees you as a babysitter, but that time with your children is time gained. A strong factor preventing her from functioning at her best is often her unresolved issues with you. She may still be preoccupied with blaming and filled with distrust that you're going to "steal" her children. Give her a copy of this book.

You make a big mistake if you let yourself get caught up in her blaming debate. As tempting as it may be to want to blame back, or react to her continuing provocations, you must learn to temper your responses, try to control them completely and, instead, offer up understanding and even kindness for the sake of your children and increasing access to them. This may seem absurd and impossible to you right now. This is the fight of your life. Nevertheless, not only can you do it if you set your mind to it, the thing you want above all else is to help your child get through these times. Approaching the mother of your children with the attitude of trying to help her manage her day and her stress will have the best results in terms of gaining time with your children and easing their transition into a split family.

Warning: Do not compromise on basic principles or put your child at risk.

Dozens of studies tell researchers that the harm done to children upon parental separation is in direct proportion to the level of stress experienced by the parent and how he/she deals with that stress. The better able you are to understand the factors that create stress in the mother, the more likely you will be able to help relieve some of it. Here I am obviously talking about a good enough parent rational enough to put the best interest of the child ahead of their own. A parent with a serious personality disorder, left unrecognized and untreated, does not fall into this category. That parent lives and breathes the illusion of righteousness and will fight to the bitter end. Pity the child brought up viewing the world through the same cracked lenses of an imbalanced parent.

A childless couple ending their relationship may never want to see each other again. That has its own misfortune but can be understood. Some parents with children who break free from the constraints of a failing relationship set out with the same desire to sever the former partner completely from their life. Sometimes that feeling results in the alienated parent abandoning their children but this behaviour is rare in both genders. Most parents will endure great hardships to remain in their children's lives and can find a way to fulfill their shared obligations by setting rules of conduct for themselves and appropriate boundaries in their interactions with the other parent.

There is wisdom in learning to turn the other cheek, over and over again if required, and just doing what it takes to make the mother a happier person. This may mean letting her think she has pulled something over you, has won this or that point or come off a disagreement feeling she is the winner. Remember, at the height of your love for her you probably let her have her way a number of times and thought it amusing. Things that may seem impossible to you now are likely things that you've done for a long time, but now you can exercise an emotional awareness and have a level of conscious decision that likely didn't exist before and that makes all the difference.

This task may be the most difficult facing you. Research tells us that the normal incidence of emotionally or mentally disturbed women in the general population increases in women who fail at a relationship. The same is true of psychological disorders. The mother of your children may be less able to deal with her new found single parent status than she thought. While she had visions of her life being made more simple and powerful she suddenly has to solve her own problems and the number of problems may have risen beyond her plans.

It's been my experience in family law that children of separated parents tend generally to have fewer parenting demands made upon them than they had before the break up. Such children also quickly learn how to manipulate their parents. If you are a non-custodial father, it is a near guarantee that you will experience new problems of parenting. It is easy to fall into the role of a good time buddy, spending money on the kids and just doing things to create fun memories. Parenting is hard under these circumstances. Discipline can cause a reaction. If your ex is alienating the children, any attempt you make to properly parent can become a complaint by the child to the mom who then spins it in court as proof that the child doesn't like you or want to be with you. That's a realistic fear but children actually appreciate and do better with structure in their lives so don't be afraid to create household rules and reinforce them. It's all about balance. To kids, a lack of structure can translate to them thinking you don't care about what they do.

Try not to think of your job as making life easier for your ex, look at it as making life easier for your children. In terms of expectations, all you have to fall back on are your experiences with her during the relationship and it becomes doubly difficult now because the break up and new stresses on her life can compound the earlier problems. If she was influenced by childhood issues, unhealthy emotional needs, and unrealistic desires during the relationship, she may now be much more seriously emotionally disturbed. Couple this with the likelihood that her available income is not enough to meet her continuing financial demands, and she is in major stress. This can have a profound negative effect on her ability to relate to you and to her responsibilities as a parent.

If you are a non-custodial parent, it is particularly frustrating – even a bit scary for some – to think that the child's future emotional health, and a great deal more, may be placed in the hands of a mother who is functioning well below where she should be. You have two choices: Fight in court to get more time and control of and with your child, or lean over backward to help the mother recover. Leaving a child with a mother who poses emotional and potential physical risks to your children is never a desirable course of action.

If you are dealing with someone who is not a fit parent you must fight for the well-being of your children, but try to remember that the well-being of their mother is also in their best interests and keep your mind open to the ways in which you can help her restore her equilibrium if she poses a threat to your children. Everyone agrees children benefit from having access to both parents so where you can help the mother become more fit you should try to do so.

Change causes stress and divorce is one of the most stressful events in the lives of all involved. Where change is perceived as a loss in life circumstances, stress grows. Try to promote the new circumstances as a good thing. The proverbial glass as half full because there is no more fighting instead of half empty because everyone is not in the same house. Every defeat or bad turn should be seen as an opportunity to learn and grow. Instead of being away from their normal friends, the second house can be a chance to double the friendship groups. Focus on how these changes can enhance your child's life and show them that you care about the things that are important to them. Helping them adapt without a sense of loss will be challenging but in the process you can learn more about your child that you would have otherwise. Let them know you care about their thoughts and feelings and validate their concerns when they trust you enough to share their thoughts and feelings. Don't take it personally if they are angry they missed a birthday party or if they miss one of their friends because they are with you instead.

Children are affected in different ways when their parents separate. They all suffer. Some pull through it without too much ill effect. Most have a hard time. Still others suffer serious and often long lasting effects. For many children, the actual separation is just one more chapter in what has been a progressively worsening situation for some time. For others it comes as a complete surprise. Children are resilient. If you pay attention to what they are experiencing, they'll come out okay. If the mother is acting destructively and putting the children at emotional risk that makes your job even more important. Set aside your anger when your children are with you and be their guide post.

With minor exception, conflict-oriented mothers have one legal arm outstretched seeking money while the other clutches their children tight, suffocating them and blind to their suffering. While money is never a minor issue with fathers, with very minor exception children are the top priority for men in litigation. Some judges will grant the mother more money from the father than the evidence and rules would otherwise suggest in a form of exchange for granting him more access. Baby for bucks barter. Get ready for it. Remember the priority is your children. This is a tough part of negotiations but enter the battle with an open heart and mind. This is not a battle about money, this is a disagreement about children. Show the judge your heart is in the right place.

CHAPTER 13: A NEW GIRL

A particularly difficult dilemma to resolve is the new girlfriend phenomenon. There is no stronger anti-depressant than the attention, sympathy, and affection of a caring woman. No finer drug to calm the anxiety, massage the abandonment fears, stroke the manhood ego, and pull a recently separated man from a dark well of self-doubt. A hot new affair is a quick fix no different than the dope a junkie needs to shoot in his arm. You can become addicted quickly to sex, or booze, or work – anything to keep your mind off the job at hand: solving the problem with your children and their mother and dealing with the hard work of healing.

If you had no child you would be free to jump right in on a rebound relationship or start playing the field as you see fit. As a father, you do not have that luxury. Resist the temptation. Your child needs your undivided love and attention more than ever right now. It is difficult enough for a child to suddenly have an absent parent and fear the loss of that love. For that child to see or even think you have a new girlfriend would be salt on a very open wound.

When you do find that new someone special, keep her as a separate part of your life until the two of you both conclude that you have what it takes to enter into a long-term relationship. When the time is right, and you have established commitment to each other, gradually introduce her into the children's lives. This process takes a great deal of finesse. Where possible, tell your children's mother yourself. Don't let her hear it from the kids. But tell the kids first. Don't let them hear from their mother.

It is not good for children to see their parents separate and one or both of them jump right away into another serious relationship. It is especially harmful for kids to get sucked into this new relationship only to have it collapse as well. Serial monogamy on the part mothers is really harmful. Without caution your children will see love and relationships as fleeting and unstable and may create trouble for them when trying to form their own relationships when they are older. It is for very good reason that everyone who has knowledge of the subject advises men not to seriously date for at least eighteen months or, even better, two years. Wait out the grieving period for the loss of your relationship and learn to be confident as a single father.

Mothers often have their attorney put a clause in a separation agreement that forbids the father from bringing a new woman into the child's life. It would be nice to think that the mother has only the best interests of the child at heart by inserting such a condition, and sometimes that is the case. More often it is a tactic of control motivated by jealousy or fear of your child getting to know what a healthy and more normal woman can be like. If this is a condition your ex is asking for, focus on how long the time frame will be and approach the condition as something you plan on as a proper parenting concern. Romantic relationships, as you have learned, are a lot of energy. Right now you need to devote that energy to your children.

If and when you do find a new partner, her role is extremely important and comes with many challenges. A new fiancée or wife and step-mother can provide enormous stability for both yours and your children's lives. If your ex is still on the warpath it can be unimaginably difficult on the new woman. Even the best of these women can find it too much to bare. On top of your ex trying to keep the children away from you, having her drive your fiancée away as well can be maddening beyond belief. Here you must exercise Herculean cool.

While professional custody and access evaluators may be more impressed by a stable, intelligent woman who has bonded with you than their impression of the natural mother, this should not be seen as a tactic in a competition. Your new girlfriend is not the mother of your children and shouldn't be promoted as such. She will never be their real mother, no matter how much your children may like her. While a stable, intelligent, and educated woman might help as a witness to harmful behaviour your ex has exhibited, she can do so as a supportive new friend and should not be presented as a replacement for the mother.

In 2006, the U.S. Census Bureau found that 60% of second marriages and 73% of third marriages end in divorce. What your children need is stability and a healthy understanding of a loving relationship. Your children don't care if your new girlfriend looks like a supermodel or if she runs her own business. She is not their mother. As they get older and they have adapted to the divorce, they will hopefully want to see you fall in love with someone again but they're not going to appreciate the "honeymoon" experience of a new girlfriend in your life too soon. If you are only having every other weekend visitations as a secondary parent, a new woman in the house is just stealing time from the precious moments you have with your kids.

Whatever romantic relationships you might take on while going through your divorce, do so with discretion and choose someone who understands the space you need while helping your children through the divorce. It will be a rare woman.

The Prophet, by Kahlil Gibran:

Your children are not your children.

They are the sons and daughters of Life's longing for itself.

They come through you but not from you,

And though they are with you yet they belong not to you.

You may give them your love but not your thoughts,

For they have their own thoughts.

You may house their bodies but not their souls,

For their souls dwell in the house of tomorrow,

which you cannot visit, not even in your dreams.

You may strive to be like them,

but seek not to make them like you.

For life goes not backward nor tarries with yesterday.

You are the bows from which your children

as living arrows are sent forth.
The archer sees the mark upon the path of the infinite,
and He bends you with His might
that His arrows may go swift and far.
Let your bending in the archer's hand be for gladness;
For even as He loves the arrow that flies,
so He loves also the bow that is stable.

CHAPTER 14:   TO RECONCILE OR NOT

An extremely small percentage of couples who separate under extremely antagonistic circumstances miraculously reconcile. Nobody seems to know exactly what indicators or traits result in this turn of events. Waiting times to file for divorce are put in place exactly because many couples return to the relationship after a year or two apart. In most cases, there was a good reason you split up in the first place. Despite the desire to spare the children from a divorce, the decision to reconcile should be considered carefully.

Many men desire to be perceived as reasonable and remain open to reconciliation to avoid being seen as the "bad guy" who wouldn't compromise. A choice to reconcile should include careful consideration of how the relationship is affecting you mentally and physically and whether or not the problems have been sufficiently addressed or even capable of being addressed. Don't engage in discussion of reconciliation where you are merely trying to get the other person to admit it's over first. There are many ways to act responsibly, and maturely, without placing yourself back into a relationship that is unhealthy. If your ex has truly come to feel attracted to you again then she will show the truth of this by considering all the options. Your children will not benefit from ongoing argument and repeat breakups. Whatever the future holds, it should be something you feel is sustainable and solid.

At the very least, if your ex wants to meet with you to discuss getting back together document it so that if she returns to claims that you are abusive you'll have evidence that she is exaggerating her claims. You can suggest or agree to some form of counseling. Be careful to interview the therapist to make sure they have a balanced gender perspective before agreeing to sessions.

Don't feel guilty about moving forward, even if your ex

claims she's still in love with you. The only people you have responsibility to are your children and yourself. Be very cautious about jumping back into a marriage that may not have changed at all. Your children need stability, not a home that keeps breaking up and reforming in an endless cycle of disrepair. While part of you might wish to go back to happier times, a reconciliation will never go back. It must be built on new terrain. Both people must have changed in some way that will make the marriage stronger if it has a chance of working.

Whatever choice you make, do so in strength not weakness. Keep focused on the future.

Guilt may make you regret you took that final step and separated. This is very common. Everyone, after abandoning any serious endeavor, thinks of many ways they might have been able to make it last, or how they could have and should have done better. In most cases, there is no singular moment that made or broke the relationship. It is an issue of personalities and compatibility. Declarations of love don't make differences disappear.

The point I am driving at is this: if you and the mother of your child had what it takes to get back together the odds are you wouldn't be heading to court in an adversarial position in the first place. Think about it: do you really want to go back to where you just escaped from? And even if you did, would she be able to change, as you will have to, to make it work the next time? It's hard enough to go through a marriage break down once. Always move forward, not backwards, and think carefully about what role your ex will play in that more positive future.

There are some dysfunctional marriages that, for purely financial reasons, one or both parents rationally decide must continue until the children are out of the home. That used to be considered upon high school or college graduation. The degree of dysfunction is not so extreme as to prevent two rational parents from entering into a peace treaty forced upon them by financial circumstances. Provided the negativity between the parents is kept to a bare minimum or not at all the arrangement can be good for the children.

CHAPTER 15: THE HIDDEN SILVER LINING

"A foolish consistency is the hobgoblin of little minds." – Ralph Waldo Emerson.

Consistency has its place in a special food recipe, kicking a field goal, and coming to work on time. We all learn to positively enjoy the predictability of our lives, our human relationships, and the world around us. We are suspicious or even fearful of change. Most of our life has been a series of putting in known inputs and getting out the expected outputs. In the process, we glue ourselves to our own unique status quo.

How then do we deal with the great truth that the only constant in life is change? Why are we not better prepared for major change when it comes?

We all enjoy the occasional pleasant surprising experiences in uncharted territory of our life. We are less prepared for unexpected and unwanted changes that are endemic to modern life. We are totally unprepared for the catastrophe of a failed relationship with the other parent of our children. This is where change can morph into chaos, uncertainty into fear.

A necessary tool to help us fear change less is to resist labeling everything we look at, hear or think about, as either good or bad, right or wrong, true or false. It is the dividing up of our thoughts, our own internal feelings, our feelings towards others, our perspective of people and things in the world, into these contrasting categories that reinforce our captivity within the status quo.

The idea here is to not look upon confusing changes in life as "disasters" but as potential opportunities. Look into your own responses and reactions to what is happening and gauge how much of its effect relates to your innate discomfort with change. With the passage of time, you can in fact look back at what has happened as being "good news". How many people do you know who, for various reasons, stayed too long and too hard in a relationship that had no future? They eventually looked back on the breakup as the best thing that ever happened to them. Someday what's happening now to you will be looked upon "as the best thing that ever happened."

Most men whose relationships have floundered on the rocky shoals of life suspect, somewhere in the recesses of their mind, that it could all be for the best. What is required is to nurture and grow that belief large enough to override the negativity which has consumed you. Help it engulf you with positive emotions that provide sustenance to strengthen your resolve to make a clean break from the past. Set your failed hero images aside. Follow your bliss on the road to discovering your soul.

Remember what all great traditions hold in common: when we find ourselves having lost our way and descend to the bottomless depths of despair, that is the very best moment to commit to a total reappraisal and approach to life. As messy and totally fucked up as your life is, now is your   unequalled   opportunity.

PART II – UNDERSTANDING YOUR EX

CHAPTER 16:   HOW YOUR EX THINKS

"Compassion is a state of mind intent on protecting others from suffering." – Gen Lamrimpa

Your children need you to have compassion for their mother. That thought may enrage you right now. Remember compassion is not the same thing as kindness, nor is it the same as sympathy. Compassion aims to alleviate suffering.

You cannot demand of someone more than they are capable of giving. To do so will only result in frustration, anger, and resentment. If your ex is irrational you cannot expect her to act rationally. If your ex is vindictive and emotionally damaged, you cannot expect her to act peacefully. If your ex is selfish you cannot expect her act generously.

Coming to a clear understanding of your ex and what she is capable of right now will not only prepare you for court, it will alleviate the stress of her hurtful actions when you understand that it is a natural product of her state of mind. Compassion towards your ex is good for your child, good for your shared family and friends, good for her and ultimately good for you. Accept the conditions that exist and you will be better able to handle the problems you are facing in your negotiations.

The failure of a loving relationship shatters many shared and personal dreams. Standing in the grave yard of broken dreams, try to put behind you any feelings of betrayal or loss. Sweep away the pieces of your life that can no longer be repaired. If your ex is not the person you thought she was, then focus on learning who she really is so that you can adjust your expectations to the new reality. Unless she is totally wacko, the courts aren't going to take the kids totally away from her. You are left as one person who can try and help her.

If the name of the game is to lesson animosity and stress and increase communication and understanding – to help you both be better parents – then caring about her dreams is important, even if you feel she gives a rat's ass about yours. Maybe her dream is to claim all your resources for herself while she moves on to another relationship having you pay for those dreams and blocking all access to your children. Caring about her dreams doesn't mean supporting them. Working on communicating with your ex will arm you with the knowledge of her plans. The less you react emotionally to what she tells you, the better able you will be to identify where her new "dreams" do not align with your own.

How do you get to a place where you can remain calm even if she tells you that she's going to make you her financial slave to support "her" kids. Well, practice thinking something helpful toward her the next time a negative thought or image of her pops up in your mind. What can you do, in some small way, to help her come up with a plan that doesn't involve harming you or the children? You can only do your best. Nevertheless, unless you are granted sole custody, your children will still be spending significant amounts of time with their mother. If you can help bring more stability to her home, then everyone will benefit.

Many couples with children end a relationship on amicable grounds and remain, if not friends, at least cordial and civil with each other. Even respectful. The children of such couples are very fortunate. The negative impact on their lives will be considerably less than on those children whose separated parents fail to emotionally and psychologically disengage from the troubles of their past.

Unresolved issues or pathologies of the mother feeding on-going disputes between you both can cause you to respond reflexively without first thinking about how or if you should respond at all. Knowing what to respond to and what not to respond to and how to choose your actions is important. Serious time and attention should be spent on coming to a clear understanding of emotional triggers and how to avoid them. Being in a state of constant readiness (or fear) of her next attack, or being obsessively concerned with how to fight back, is a stress factor which can negatively affect your mental and physical health. Always walking on egg shells is nerve racking. Remaining engaged with her at this level may feed her need for conflict and reward her poor behavior. Some tragic women are fueled by the need for constant combat. Just because you don't get the desired results from trying to help, don't quit on her.

Both mothers and fathers can get caught up spending far too much time and mental energy trying to score a cheap shot or scheming how to get even when they are wronged. These skirmishes drag the children onto the battlefield causing deep and lasting damage. It takes self-awareness and strong discipline to extract oneself from this mutually destructive dynamic. It also requires you to have a highly intelligent understanding of the tangled emotional roots that shaped her personality. Tragically, many such mothers have little if any insight into their own motivations.

Anyone who has ever had any experience in mediation or negotiating knows the difference between a person's staked out position on a subject and the underlying concerns, fears, or values which dictate the stated position. The stated position may mask the unstated deeper concerns.

A mother's stated position on custody may be that the children will be cared for better if completely in her care. The actual underlying motive may have nothing to do with parenting skills. She may just be fearful of not being able to maintain her lifestyle without the child support payments that come with having custody. She may not want to be seen by her support group as incapable as a single mother. If she is surrounded by other single mothers hung up in continuing antagonism with the fathers of their children, there may be social pressure for her to exaggerate your "dark side." They may be convincing her that she was being abused. More typically it is as simple as fear the child may love the father more than her.

Where the stated positions of the mother stem from

deep emotional scars, no amount of rational response is going to have any effect. Any kind of response to such women may merely feed their warped sense of control. They gain strength by drawing an emotional reaction from you and it makes no difference what the response is. For such women, the tragic reality of their life is that the only certainty they have come to rely upon is the fight – they live for it. Parenting becomes a contest between you and her and the contest becomes a part of her lifestyle. Sending e-mails or letters pleading with the mother to "think about the children" or "please be fair" is worse than useless when you are dealing with someone who enjoys a fight. It is the fuel that feeds and sustains her combat When you get sucked in to responding it only confirms she still has you under her emotional control. When you learn not to respond you deny her emotional sustenance you are breaking the codependency she has established or is trying to breed.

With such mothers you have to limit your communications to the bare essentials of only information required for the proper parenting of the children, namely schedules, events, appointments, school information, etc.

On the other hand, where the stated position of the mother is a true statement of a legitimate concern, and is not masking some underlying psycho-dynamic, addressing her concerns can build a bridge. Such communications can put forward your views and opinions on the issues, and comment politely on her views whether you agree or disagree. Avoid a tone which is argumentative, accusing or demeaning, even if you are hurt by her lack of trust in you or your character. If she legitimately holds these opinions, then it would be useful to recognize her perceptions of you and address her concerns in a productive way.

The statutes on family law in many jurisdictions direct a judge, when considering custody, to consider whether there has been abuse in the relationship. Legal aid programs often make claims of abuse mandatory if the applicant mother is going to be provided with a lawyer for free. Where such legislation exists, the incidents of mothers "fleeing" to battered women shelters increases. A term in prison for a young thief can be an education into becoming a better thief. A non-abused mother joining other non-abused mothers in shelters is a finishing school for victimhood.

CHAPTER 17: BELIEF VS REASON

Mothers with deep-seated, undiagnosed personality disorders can often function well and go undetected in marriage and society. When their marriage collapses they find themselves rejected, alone and afraid. These sympathetic individuals have to create an illusory world to salvage their sense of self purpose. In varying degrees of delusion, they reinvent themselves as the sole parent capable of protecting their child. Having, keeping, and never sharing their child can become their sole goal in life. The child becomes the provider of the emotional support the mother requires to sustain herself. I call that emotional incest. A healthy mother child bond is where the parent is the emotional support for the child, not the other way around.

This dynamic emerges from the unconscious realms of her mind and manifest itself in her conscious mind as an independent belief system. The belief comes with a full tool kit of distorted memories, exaggerated emotions, and a history of false facts, all which elevate and justify her as the required parent. The father is at best a wallet to support the mother and at worst a danger to the child's wellbeing.

The mother's belief system is immune from reason and facts. In this regard, it is similar to any irrational religious belief founded in faith. It is impervious to reason. By her definition it can't be challenged. Often when push comers to shove, and all her alleged factual reason are proven false, she falls back on a claim of "mother's intuition."

CHAPTER 18:   RECOGNIZING ABUSE

There was a time not so long ago when you married someone to share a home, be a parent, have occasional sex, and hope that a lasting love would result. That constituted marital satisfaction. Somewhere over the years an added expectation appeared: Personal growth.

Somewhere along the way, people have developed this idea that your spouse should help meet and fulfill your psychological needs. (To be a modern mate you are expected to develop a spiritual or even psychic connection in which you should be able to read the mind of your spouse.) To the extent that those psychological needs were healthy, realistic, and capable of being met, this expectation may not cause terminal problems. Strong relationships are built between whole people. But there is no "better half" to someone who is incomplete and insecure. I could not tell you the number of times a father has come into my office and told me that his wife has just announced she needs to "discover herself" and she can only do so outside of the marriage. While the woman feels her inner self has been stifled by her partner's lack of proper attention, you'll inevitably note in these scenarios that she has not concerned herself with whether or not her spouse has achieved or has a need for any self-actualization in the relationship.

The "self-help" aisles in the new age book stores, together with the pop psychology magazine racks and TV shows, bear witness to the gigantic industry spawned by this phenomenon. The grievance industry and oppression Olympics make top dollar by convincing women they are being abused. While their lack of emotional care for their partner, lack of understanding for the pressures and problems he deals with every day, and their occasional verbal or physical outbursts are seen as proper responses to difficult situations, the husband is seen as "coercively controlling," and neglectful. His efforts at self-defense in a physical assault are seen as "male violence."

Divorce rates have climbed, in major part, because of one single fact: day to day dissatisfaction and general unhappiness has been transformed into some kind of abuse. Modern day therapists contribute to this transformation of regular human emotions into signs of abuse to the point of overlooking an actual disorder in their patient. They blame it on a society that keeps women from succeeding instead of a problem with the woman herself.

If you've had a partner struggling with an undiagnosed personality disorder, you may have been just as oblivious to the extent of the mental disorder as she was. Over time, a growing anxiety and suspicion develops when efforts to alleviate the symptoms fail. You find yourself always on edge and thinking her anger or depression would make sense if only you could figure out what you did that sets her off. Even when you realize that her problems are independent from anything you have done, it may be impossible to get her to see that the problem isn't you.

When an ill partner does not admit to needing help, the relationship collapses. Children suffer. The courts get involved. Rationality goes out the window. It is the worst sort of nightmare for the healthy parent trying to regain or maintain some sense of stability to the home. A perfect storm.

Advanced techniques of investigation, modern diagnostic tools, and continuing research into the electrical/chemical make-up of the human brain have provided the mental health fields with a growing understanding of human behavior. And with it greater recognition of maladaptive behavior. Some of these undesired behaviors are categorized as personality disorders. When carefully examined it is clear that more of the general population than previously thought have personality disorders of varying types and degrees. These disorders contain elements of delusion.

"We think of delusion as the biasing by emotion of perception and cognition. Delusion involves the influence of the emotional circuits of the brain on the circuits of the brain responsible for perceiving things or apprehending the world, and also circuits that are involved in thought. These are influences that obscure our capacity to perceive realty. They reflect how emotion disrupts both our perception and our thinking." – Richard Davidson "Destructive Emotions: A Scientific Dialogue With the Dalai Lama", by Daniel Goleman.

These delusion-causing disorders can range from bipolar to borderline personality disorder. Personality disorder delusions are not the same as schizophrenic caused delusions. Women are afflicted with borderline personality disorder considerably more often than men. These and other disorders, where they exist, will prevent a mother from understanding and approaching the break-up and its aftermath in a rational way. Such individuals are less able to resolve disputes and are more likely to end up in the court system making unreasonable demands which will harm their children.

Mothers who suffer from borderline or narcissistic disorders, resulting from poor parenting and tragic experiences in their own childhood, may never gain meaningful insight into the cause of their troubles. The dysfunctional relationship between her and your child is unhealthy and may never improve. As the child's only healthy parent, you will have to find a way to come to find peace and effective ways of working around the problem. Essentially, your children will need you even more.

Just as it's easy to self-diagnose yourself with every disorder you read about, be wary of thinking you are a psychiatrist who has figured out the problems of your ex. Remember that the long lists of behaviors and symptoms you may read about are, on their own, fairly generic. While you may feel you have pinpointed a mental illness that explains your ex's behaviour, your diagnosis is not meaningful or useful to a judge. But your detailed description of her behavior is vitally important.

Where there is a proper diagnosis by a qualified practitioner and an acknowledgment of an illness, show compassion but insistence that the disorder be addressed in terms of your children's safety.

A common phenomena and fact pattern in family court is this:

The behaviour of a parent – either parent – that is reprehensible and harming to the child is agreed by all involved in the trial to be a threat to the child's best interests. Unless the ill parent had a pre-court encounter with Jesus and makes full confession you may not be able to identify the concerns you have with her mental stability by name but you can address the specific behaviors that have caused your concern.

If the examples are plain, and the deviant parent remains unaware of or in denial of her behavior, it will bolster your position. If you are expressing serious concerns about the safety of your children be sure the complaints are based on evidence and are not trivial. Have witnesses where possible, and introduce the concerns with focus on concerns for the children and not on anger at the events.

More commonly, you may be the target of abuse allegations yourself where your ex has willfully fabricated events that never took place or launched a campaign of denigration, even employing your own children against you in the ruse. These allegations may be enhanced or twisted versions of real events or may be manufactured completely. If this is the case, it is scary. You may be fighting panic and unable to focus on how to prove yourself innocent. Where there are allegations of sexual and/or physical violence you may need legal representation.

The key problem in dealing with personality disordered women in court is that few psychologists or psychiatrists want to go on record labelling a mother to be as mentally ill as they actually believe she is. This is a serious flaw in the so called justice system.

Getting a full, expert evaluation of an ex-wife's pathology is expensive. If that doesn't end the litigation, then a full trial must follow at an astronomical expense for the average working person. While physical abuse is easier to document, mental and emotional abuse is difficult to prove, especially when the complaint is against the mother. While you may be convinced that your ex has a mental illness, avoid naming it in court unless you are prepared to prove it. Instead, focus on the acts and the attitudes that you can back up with evidence.

If it took you years to figure out you were being emotionally abused, don't expect a judge to figure it out in a day or week.

While physical abuse is more easily recognized, it often is merely an escalation of the underlying emotional or psychological abuse being inflicted. Men who have been routinely subjected to low level physical abuse often don't recognize it. They have just figured over the years that the occasional push, slap, shove, scratch, or outright punch from their partner is part of the deal. As the man, you are not supposed to complain but simply learn to put up with it. If you are somewhat co-dependent, you will make it your task to suffer the abuse valiantly and make it your mission to help her stop doing it.

Continuing research documents that women and men are equal opportunity abusers.

If you have been abused over a long period of time, you will get needed comfort by realizing that you are by no means alone. You can get help on recovering from its effects. The more pernicious effects of systemic emotional abuse are to trap you in a false vision of yourself created by your spouse (and/or her family) to suit her manipulative needs. You can't begin to discover who you really are and what sort of person you could become when trapped inside this fictitious self. The longer you've been subjected to her abuse the longer it will take to break the cycle.

For men, it can be embarrassing to admit when you've been abused. Attempts to tell others can be met with mockery or disdain. Gender stereotypes and myths stand as a barrier to men seeking help for what others may see as a weakness. There are a growing number of men who are speaking out and offering support for other men who have found themselves in this position. These same stereotypes are part of the reason men will put up with abuse for so long. They want to be seen as supportive, "good" men with the strength to stand by their woman even when she is causing them pain.

If you have been abused by a woman and want to engage with activists who have created support groups for men, keep in mind many men who have not dealt properly with their own issues can end up being counterproductive in their help of others. While it is wonderful to take part in father's support groups, the best activists are those who have worked through their issues, understood and dealt with their anger, frustration, and abuse, and their divorce is in the past. If you want to share your experiences with others, do so in a way that focuses on healing and keeps you in a balanced frame of mind to deal with your most pressing issue: resolving the divorce, amicably if possible.

A man who has suffered through years of subtle or not so subtle emotional abuse from the woman he loved is a sorrowful figure. More often than not he has lost not only the ability to extract himself from the relationship and seek professional help where necessary, he sometimes doesn't even see ending the relationship as a good in itself. He may be guilt ridden and completely under the thumb of the woman who has convinced him that everything that goes wrong is his fault. He may be more focused on a sense of failed duty, instilled by his wife, than on recognizing ways in which his confidence and autonomy was being undermined.

While men tend to have physical advantages over women in both size and strength, when it comes to emotional engagement of a competitive nature, it's my belief that women can beat us nearly every time.

Workshops with men and women talking about the strengths and weaknesses of their own gender and the strengths and weaknesses of the other gender, always conclude that women are the subtler, stealthy, and emotionally persistent aggressor whenever they wish to be. This is seen nowhere more accurately than in relationships between men and women that are not based on an equality of respect, and equality of need, and an equality of power. Men tend to be more direct during disputes and, when they are angry or frustrated they will make it known clearly. Because men don't tend to create long term plans of emotional subjugation they don't recognize this type of game and can be under attack for many years having no idea what caused the aggression or how it was being played out.

The Man Myth

Of the many myths that stalk the halls of justice in our society one of the most ill-conceived is that men are the violent sex and women are meek, mild, and never aggressive. Until the 1990s, the statistics that proved neither gender has a monopoly on peaceful behavior were hidden for literally decades. There are some facts the organs of society charged with educating the public don't want to give out. This has been a big one.

We now know women physically abuse men just about as often as men abuse women, only they do it differently. On the other hand, I think women emotionally abuse men much more effectively than men can emotionally abuse or manipulate women. Physical abuse by wives against husbands is harmful in its direct impact, but more damaging in how it leaves the man feeling about himself is emotional abuse. Some men believe the myth our culture has perpetuated about them being the violent sex. They struggle with the dissonance when they find themselves on the opposite end. An abused man feels isolated. He feels the scorn from all levels of society.

It is important for such a man to realize that he is not alone.

Men are the victims of emotional abuse much more than the public suspects. The abuse comes in varying degrees of severity. In some cases, a woman may have completely imposed her own version of reality on the man. When this "remaking" of his vision of the world takes place he may even be fooled enough to see it as his own image of himself. Over time, men come to suppress and deny their inner dreams and ambitions while constructing a mask to conform with their partner's idea of what a "real man" and a father should look like.

Part of the process you are now going through is to realize that you haven't lost the ability to be happy, you've just lost the previous sources of your happiness. You can choose to remain forever sullen, defeated and depressed, or you can consciously pick up the pieces of learning how to find happiness within yourself again. You will discover newer sources of happiness, both internal and external, with the main one being the super joy of feeling and knowing who you are based on your own vision and focused on your own goals again. Instead of seeking support from a new woman, you can learn to be whole on your own, set proper boundaries in your relationships and improve your relationship with your children at a time when they need you more than ever.

Women Who Hit

Say the words "spousal abuse" and every one assumes men abusing women. When a man says he has been physically assaulted by his wife he is met with disbelief. He must have deserved it. Perhaps it was in self-defense. How is that possible? He is so much bigger than she is. Data suggests men and women abuse each other about evenly, but differently. They threaten violence about equally. Because women are historically more believable, and have state sponsored shelters and programs to help, they report more than men. Men under report to avoid the stigma of being regarded as a cry baby. The statistics on how often men assault women have to be seriously warped when one considers the rash of false allegations in the mother's playbook to deny children time with their fathers.

CHAPTER 19: FALSE ALLEGATIONS AND SEXUAL TOUCHING

The new trump card in the deck of desperate mothers out for revenge against the fathers of their young daughters is to passively allege sex abuse. In innocent conversations, the child mentions daddy touched her bum. The mother doesn't phone dad and find out what that was all about. Never mind he was applying cream to a rash. Child protection officials and the police are immediately called. Dad gets that most feared of all calls: the mother of your daughter has filed a complaint. "Until we investigate you can't see your daughter." Usually they leave you stunned and hanging, not telling you the nature of the complaint. Right here social workers become complicit in this pernicious act.

Days can go by before the father is told that the allegation is no more serious than after a bath he touched the child's bottom. But he still can't see his child. More investigations are required. Delay, delay, delay. By this time the mother has cranked it up drama to child abuse sufficient to deny access and have lawyers demand expensive professional supervision.

Meanwhile the confused child is missing her daddy. She is shuffled around to pokers and prodders and strange interrogators. A regular inquisition. "What has daddy done so wrong that they won't let me see him?" This is the prime time for alienating mothers to insinuate various degrees of brainwashing into the innocent young mind. Social works, lawyers and judges remain oblivious to what is happening to the child, and by so doing, become complicit in the harm to her. They lean over backwards apologizing to the father for the inconvenience. Judges politely warn the mother that if it all turns out to be a false alarm she will have a penalty to pay. Such faint praise is just so much salt in his wound. And there can be no greater wound to a man.

By the time the appropriate authorities declare false alarm, and the daughter is released back to her father, what happens to the mother? Absolutely nothing. Sending the police on a wild goose case is mischief and is a criminal offense. Does the offending mother ever get charged? Never. Do the courts remove the child from her or even give the dad more time? Never. Does the promised judicial penalty materialize? Never.

Does dad ever fully recover from the malevolent allegation? Never.

These mothers fall into two camps: those who are sufficiently personality disordered to project everything possible of a horrible nature onto the father in the full belief of its truth. And those who don't believe it but fly with it to gain financial advantage – i.e. custody and child support.

These lawyers retained by these dysfunctional mothers pocket their fees, rationalizing their collaboration in injuring the child and defaming the father as just another day at the office and go home to their kids.

CHAPTER 20:   PARENTIAL ALIENATION

Parental alienation – the concerted attempt by one parent to fracture the bond of a child with the other parent – is child abuse of the worst kind. It should be a criminal offense.

Parental alienation is a pernicious form of abuse too often given only lip service by the courts. Alienators, historically camouflaged and augmented by gender politics, have hoodwinked psychologists and judges for too long. Current data, knowledge, and research demand a more concerted exposure and recognition of this type of abusive parent. The dynamic involved in serious parental alienation is a very complex one even for psychologists to understand. We need strengthened resolve on the part of judges to understand and pay heed to the growing number of experts in this field.

Children hearing one parent say bad things about the other is as old as language itself. Parents incorporating negatives in a purposeful campaign to damage or prevent a bond between their child and the other parent is primarily a late twentieth-century phenomenon. As the mid- to late 20th century 'tender years doctrine,' giving preference to mothers, gave way to concerns for the best interests of the child, false allegations of sex abuse became more common.

The cause and effect is clear: when an unjustified, gender based claim by a mother for sole custody no longer guaranteed the result sought, out came the trump card: sex abuse! When the courts and health care professionals eventually disclosed the high incidents of false allegations, serious attempts (and successes) at parental alienation increased. This was the new silver bullet. When a child shows extreme prejudice against and dislike of one parent during assessment, the mother's claims for sole custody are more likely to be granted. Initially it was predominantly mothers who alienated, but seeing the success it offered, fathers are starting to adopt the tactic.

No loving parent would ever put his children through this form of abuse, even when they fear they is being victimized by this approach.

Columbia University child psychiatrist Dr. Richard Gardner pioneered the public debate with his book Parental Alienation Syndrome. His thesis was as simple as it has become controversial: An extreme campaign of alienation by a parent can cause the child to exhibit a common set of symptoms. These include:

• A campaign of denigration

• Weak, absurd, or frivolous rationalizations for the deprecation

• Lack of ambivalence

• The "independent-thinker" phenomenon

• Reflexive support of the alienating parent in the parental conflict

• Absence of guilt over cruelty to and/or exploitation of the alienated parent

• The presence of borrowed scenarios

• Spread of the animosity to the friends and/or extended family of the alienated parent

Gardner argued that the collectivity of these symptoms indicate a psychiatric break from reality in the mind of the child. The symptoms constitute a syndrome, which he called "Parental Alienation Syndrome (PAS)." The continuing debate over whether alienation can be a syndrome or should be seen as a psychiatric disorder in the child serves mainly to take the court's eye off the ball. Even Gardner's most strident critics acknowledge that Gardner's list of symptoms can be found in most cases.

In the years since Gardner brought needed focus to the problem, accredited professionals have nuanced the definitions and approaches to the condition. Today, there are multifaceted approaches to recognizing that the factors contributing to PAS can be more than just one parent's vendetta against the other parent. Journal articles, text, and popular books and untold web sites abound on the subject. An increasing number of psychologists in child assessment have made PAS a sub-specialty.

Similar to individuals with borderline personality disorder, serious alienators are masters at masking their actions by hiding behind a façade of personal and social charm and acceptability. They are often supremely convincing to any person, even professionals such as lawyers or judges who have had no previous experience with the disorder.

The first defense taken up by an accused alienator is that the child's rejection of the other parent is based on actual faults of the target parent. Knowing that changing custody of the child is often the recommended first step in countering serious parental alienation, the alienating parent, when confronted, becomes one of the most dishonest witnesses to ever take the stand. Typically, their naïve lawyer is right there holding their hand. If the lawyer is a victim feminist herself, she is the mother's cheering section.

An early victim of the alienator's fictionalized version of events is often their own lawyer: hook, line, and proverbial sinker. Another victim is the counselor or psychologist who is brought on board to help the child when it is the parent who needs the help. A major part of the problem is the continuing mistake on the part of judges to direct counseling or supervised visits between the child and the target parent. Defining the problem between the child and the target parent is exactly what the alienating parent and their lawyer hope for: keeping all eyes off the alienating parent.

The trial judge is often the final and most significant victim. Inexperience in their personal lives, inexperience on the bench, wanting to see the good in a parent, particularly in a mother, too quick to judge the father, produces the most important enabler for the alienating process. Worst of all, when a judge agrees that there is sever alienation, they haven't got the intelligence and fortitude to take the child from the alienator and give the child to the target parent. This is the most frustrating part of these trials. Months and months even years of work and money only to have the judge slap the child abusing parent on the wrist and say "please don't do it anymore."

If there is no local psychologist whose specialty is parental alienation, find an outside expert. When you bring concerns about parental alienation to the case, demand that it be taken seriously and investigated properly.

1. Diagnosing a parent as an alienator is the first task and the first challenge.
2. Because the claim needs to be taken seriously, have your case for the existence of the syndrome laid out with care and precision. There must be convincing evidence, beyond just your claim.

3. Document specific examples of how your child's attitude toward you has changed since the separation or leading up to it. Record, by whatever means possible, how the child expresses their dislike of you especially when their anger is expressed without context or "out of the blue."

4. Pay close attention and document whenever your child makes specific references to things the mother has said about you. Do not ask the child what the mother is saying about you, just pay attention and record the moments when they offer you the information independently. Remember that you are focused on helping your child and you want to avoid placing them in the middle of the battle. They are the biggest victims in parental alienation and must always be the focus of primary concern.

5. The most difficult task is deciding what to do for the child involved. A parental alienation expert can assist a judge to evaluate the evidence and recommend options for repairing the damage.

Engage With Experts

The unresolved psychological or childhood issues of parents of either gender are often contributing factors to the collapse of a relationship. Where it is the mother who has a fractured sense of herself, she often has a physical as well as an emotional need to keep the kids excessively close to her. She uses the kids as psychological supports to keep her self-image from total collapse.

This regression by the mother to an earlier, almost child-like existence, which may be contributed to by an actual personality disorder, is the toughest factor militating against your children. Dealing with it can consume and ruin some men. It ruins too many children.

In the face of an alienating or angry, jealous or embittered mother, it is always important for the father, if he can afford it, to keep experts working to help. It is often not possible to force the person most in need of therapy – in this case, the mother – into getting help. Judges think nothing of ordering fathers into recommended programs as a condition for access but very rarely do women get that sort of equal treatment.

If you are heading into a legal battle with an alienating parent, try to get one judge seized of your file who will hear all the applications leading up to the trial. Otherwise, you will find yourself having to reeducate every new judge you are in front of.

Try to prepare your documentation as simply as possible and begin each time by mentioning these concerns and any validation you've received on this issue from previous applications or reviews. This is especially the case if you are unable to keep one judge who will commit to following up on your case.

Parental Alienation Hit by Hit

The early symptoms of alienation in a child can be very subtle and difficult to detect. The target parent initially has only vague suspicions, experienced as a shudder in the soul. Above almost all else in the diminished or lost role as a parent is the horrible fear that the other parent has commenced a campaign to sabotage the bond between you and your child. But the signs are fleeting at first. Who is going to believe you? What judge is going to make an order that will prevent slippage? Lawyers, health care professionals and judges are not trained or experienced in recognizing the initial signs.

For how many years did brain damage to football players go unrecognized and denied? Millions were spent by the National Foot Ball League to refuting the very existence of chronic traumatic encephalopathy (CTE). CTE is a progressive degenerative disease found in people who have had repeated blows to the head. Only when players started going crazy and dying did the world wake up.

Parental alienation has the same manner of causation as CTE. Repeated and targeted slights by the alienating parent against the target parent in the presence of the child work against the parent-child bond until it frays and breaks. Like an undetected cancer, by the time it is recognized as malignant, if it is not too late, radical surgery is required.

Doctors are trained to send a patient to a specialist on the mere suspicion of a potentially serious ailment. Judges are trained to only deal with provable diagnosis. They reject a soundly based suspicion and dismiss the application with costs against the target parent.

Only the rare psychologist doing a family evaluation will address the target parent's suspicion with the respect it deserves.

CHAPTER 21: AUTISM

Mothers who seek to prevent their children from having a relationship with their father have historically utilized various tactics. False allegations of sex abuse have been around for a long time and is still a tactic. Alienating a child against the father is another. With the startling increase in autism in children over the past few decades, I have noticed a similar increase in the number of mothers who are using a child's autism to deny time with the father.

The new mantra is that the autistic child's needs for stability and predictability require one home, on bedroom, one helper with homework, and one routine with the mother. While the needs of severely autistic children might support that argument, mothers are making it with high-functioning autistic children. Child psychiatrists support shared parenting for autistic children where both parents are on the same page for home- and school-based programs.

The dynamic of autism illustrates a distinction between two categories of parents: those who have committed themselves, consciously and unconsciously, to diminish the bond between their child and the other parent for their own unmet emotional needs with disregard to the child, and those parents legitimately concerned with the needs of their child.

False allegations of sex abuse and parental alienation estrangement from a parent are fictitious devices, created and invented by the alienating parent. Autism is a diagnosable illness. It is real. Where a particular child falls on the spectrum between mild and sever is open to debate and determination.

Healthy maternal instinct can motivate a mother to argue her mild to moderately autistic child should be parented primarily by her post separation. Initial theories of treatment promoted this belief. This parent becomes less sympathetic when she starts to irrationally reject current medical expertise that supports her child being able to be patented equally with its father.

PART III – COURT AND THE SYSTEM

CHAPTER 22: THE ELEPHANT IN THE COURTROOM

There is a great big elephant in the courtrooms of the land that no one wants to talk about: gender bias. Gender bias in the courts is the rotting swamp all fathers have to slog through getting from the shoals of a ship wrecked marriage to solid ground. It infects every step of the journey. It haunts every waking moment of your escape from perdition. The bias is the myth that females are inherently more nurturing, honest and decent than males. It has run so deep for so long in our culture that even if you are not caught in the court system, you can't escape its effects in everyday life.

True, the courts have come some way in putting less weight on that debunked myth. There remains much too much of what I call the judicially sanctioned kidnapping of children by mothers. While it may be a collective criticism one can properly make of judges that the system remains biased against fathers, it is hard to fault the individual judge unaware of this very subtle prejudice we are all brought up with. While judges may recoil at this analogy, gender bias was historically as deeply ingrained as racial prejudice. Both have soggy remnants that need to be dragged out into the clear light of focused heat to be shriveled and discarded like a cancer tumor.

It takes hard work and a great deal of finesse to educate your judge on gender beliefs, understandings and sense of fairness without being accusatory or blaming.

Prepare what you naturally and honestly want to say and to tell your story. Don't directly confront the judge's personality with his/her understandable bias. You can challenge what a judge does in court. You can challenge his/her reason for it with your own common sense opinion. Good judges often like to engage in an intelligent debate on what subjective decision the judge should make.

Having stated my views, in fairness I have to recognize those few enlightened men and women judges who have overcome the biases and afford their cases with a sense of fairness to children sadly lacking elsewhere. More laudable praise belongs to those rare few who can recognize the personality disorders in the tragic mothers who come before them in court.

Gender bias needs to be addressed at the beginning of any discussion on fathers and their parenting roles post separation. A lot has been written and a lot more will be written on gender bias in society and the courts.

When I used to want to start a debate at a boring gathering of lawyers and judges, or the politicians who write the laws, I would bring up the subject of the continuing gender biases against men in family law. I would suggest that one of the great legal myths of all time is that lady justice is blind and that all who come before the law are treated equally. The apologists in the crowd would be quick to point out that the language of the statutes and laws that govern all the issues in family law are gender neutral. There are no longer any presumptions in the written law or statutes favoring mothers, etc. It is the mantra for the apologists. They are technically correct. But they are missing the point: the prejudice against fathers, as stated above, is very subtle and lies deep in the minds and belief systems of the men and women whose role it is to administer the so-called gender neutral statutes. It is also in the minds of too many psychologists who advise the judges and should know better. (The role of psychologists in perpetuating bias is for another book).

I have never met a father who doesn't know in his bones such a bias exists. They feel it. A father coming into my office for the first time knows he is about to enter into an stadium where the mother is given a big handicap and he gets none.

Many men have come to my office feeling deep fear they cannot articulate. When the trial is over, those same men all admit to how naïve they were the first day they came into my office. The bias is larger and trickier than they suspected.

Every separated father has to learn to live with the fact that there may be no equal justice. It isn't magically going to get better. The goal of a father is to get through trial suffering the least injustice possible.

A word to those who not only rightly want to see the system changed but demand it occur right now, in their case! As I discuss in more detail in the next chapter, family court is certainly not a game. But the metaphor of "game" is useful to make an important point: if you don't learn to play by the key rules of the game, you are probably going to 'lose. Finish the game. Then set about changing the rule.

CHAPTER 23: RULES OF THE GAME: HOW JUDGES AND COURTS REALLY WORK

If you were playing a championship game of football, you wouldn't spend your time during the game complaining about the rules and trying to change them as the game was being played. Successful players of any sport study and know the existing rules and are prepared to play by them. Fathers caught up in the alien experience of family court, offended at what they find, do themselves great damage by wasting time, emotion, energy, and money trying to change the rules while they are struggling on the field.

Fathers understandably see the rules of court procedure and the laws governing children after separation as overly complicated, old fashioned, unfair, and biased. The laws need changing and everyone involved needs better education on the need and benefits of real shared parenting. Yes, the system cries out for overdue reform. And yes, the whole process can be extremely expensive and ineffective. It is the game the uncaring universe has forced you to play.

When tied up in litigation in family court, it's not the time to worry about reforming the system. Fathers being dealt with harshly and unfairly, suffer only so much insult before they let their frustrations distract them from the downfield goal posts. If you take your eye off the ball, run to the sidelines to try to prove to the ref that the rules aren't fair and should be changed, you will fumble the ball. It will be recovered by your opponent.

After your court case is behind you and you have had time to readjust to your new life, then you can re-enter the legal debate and work for reform of the law. In the meantime, keep your eye on the ball and play by the rules! There will be plenty of time for you to be one of those rare men who, after the legal hassles are all behind them, stay involved in trying to help other new single fathers and to work on law reform.

How To Play By The Rules

Being successful in court takes skill and luck. Most of all it takes an understanding of the theatrical nature of the process, the roles each person plays, and the stage upon which they recite their rehearsed lines. Different scripts get heard each day in family courts. Those scripts, which work for fathers standing up for their children, share certain common themes.

Success in family court requires a man to remold himself into the conforming person judges think of as deserving to remain in the lives of their children. If that remolding is insincere, it can be seen through. Remember the theme of this book is that the process by which a father undertakes that remolding is the first stage in discovering the path to self-realization. And to soul.

Rather than begrudge and resist the legal process, fathers need to take it on as an unequalled opportunity. Why? Because there is a strong and important relationship between the character roles you must learn to play for the stage of the courtroom and the actual person you hope to eventually become once this is all behind you. The two are not the same. In fact, they may be different. But the legal persona or role player you need to become can be made into an excellent practice run at eventually finding your path. You don't really have much choice in the matter. You are stuck in the legal process. You can let it defeat you, or you can take what little control is available to you and master it.

Society's Judge

Another legal myth is that judges are somehow supposed to represent the values and ethics of "society", whatever that word might mean. Where parties in our "society" cannot resolve differences, the courts are here to resolve those disputes in a way that most conforms with the social engineering that keeps our society functioning. Few myths of any type are more easily burst than this one. Judges first have to be lawyers. Law school remains the privilege of those who can afford it and have grades to get in. Judges not only come from the profession of lawyers, an elite within society that by no definition can be said to represent anyone but themselves but they come from a special part of the legal profession. They are appointed by the government. Judges (trial and appeal judges) come from a pool of lawyers that mostly made their living representing banks, insurance companies and other establishment institutions, as well as prosecutors rather than defense lawyers. Where elected, there is a bit more variety. Most fathers up against the legal system have absolutely nothing in common with the men and women who sit in judgment on the lives of their children.

No two judges hold the same values or think of identical outcomes for each and every case. Some judges are properly known as old fashioned. Some are progressive, within moderation. Some simply have no business being judges and are incompetent in family matters. So it is always a crapshoot going into court. The best you and your lawyer (if you have one) can do is frame your case and your role and lines in it to appeal to the broader upper middle ground where most judges hold their family values. Researching family law decisions your judge has made in previous cases can provide invaluable information on their thinking process and values. Always time well spent in the law libraries or on the internet.

How A Judge Will Perceive You

The simplest way to look at what a father must do to be successful and stay in the lives of his children is to view the process from where the judge sits, and to apply that perspective to your case. In short, you have to be able to produce for the judge a history of, and proposal for, the children that fits with the judge's (society's) preconception of what is in the best interest of children generally. For most judges, while it isn't quite a case of "one size fits all," there are a limited number of sizes that fit. All judges were lawyers first. Lawyers are by definition very conservative individuals with reputations to make and status to achieve. They have a fairly establishment view of what is good or bad for children. Fathers must fit into one of the limited sizes if they are to have any real chance for their children.

It is your job to understand what judges are looking for. To the extent that a father is lacking one or more important characteristic as a parent, or even has some negative aspects, his job (and his therapist's job) is to remedy that situation as much as possible before the trial date arrives.

One parent may clearly be the unfit parent and instigator of problems. In child custody cases that don't resolve at earlier levels or mediation and end up in court, very often a parent's actions has placed the child stressfully in the middle. The parents are the two face plates of a work bench vise. One face plate is fixed and stationary. The other face plate is mobile and controlled by the other parent. That parent has possession of the screw increasing or decreasing the pressure on the child squeezed in the vise.

In any high contest fight between a mother and father, the one seeking to deny fair time for the kids to the other parent is the parent with hands on the screw vise.

Where the greedy parent hasn't the strength on their own to turn the screw, their family and friends will volunteer to help.

This may be conscious or unconscious It is an interesting argument as to which of these possibilities is the blacker mark against that parent: Knowingly doing what one shouldn't, but presumably being capable of stopping it; Or not being able to stop it because it is unconscious and part of an underlying personality problem.

One of the most difficult challenges facing a parent is how to talk to children who are being alienated against them by the other parent. Alienation typically develops into situations where the children are being directly told bad things or falsehoods about the target parent and often the target parent's family. Historically alienators were nearly always mothers. Over the past several years, an increasing number of fathers have become alienators and mothers are finding themselves the target parents. There are two opposing views as to what to do and how to handle this when it becomes known to the target parent.

One school of psychological thought holds that the father should just ignore it. The rational being that if the father engages in trying to dispute and correct it with the child, the child will become inappropriately involved. It won't matter that the mother has blatantly done exactly that to the child. These psychologists naïvely tell the father just to cool it, don't respond, give the mother space and time. Hopefully whatever unresolved childhood issues she has will resolve without therapy and she will miraculously grow out of malicious ways.

This school I call the "let's hope" school. Family law lawyers, without their own personal experience with serious parental alienators, are over ripe to being influenced by this school of thought. It is the chicken shit response.

The other school – what I call the "realism" school – was best represented by renowned child psychiatrist Dr. Richard Gardner, who died in 2003. The preponderance of expert opinion has shifted to this school, yet it is just trickling down to the legal and judicial profession.

The realism school says that target parents have to deal with it and can't just let it slide. Alienators hardly ever just suddenly see the light of day and stop. The father must talk to his children. The trick is in how to do it. It must be in an honest, factual, and psychologically appropriate way. There are good books that provide this guidance.

A little antidote I always suggest is that when a child comes "for a visit" and says "Mommy (or Daddy) says you are stupid!", pull your jacket up over your head, with your fingers stretch your cheeks around a wide open mouth, make big eyes, hunch over, make like an animal, look the child in the eyes singing in a high pitched voice: "I'm stupid, I'm stupid. I am very stupid. I'm very, very stupid." By this time the child should be in hysterics. The next time the other parent tells the child you are stupid the child is going to have that image of you psychedelically zapped into her mind's eye. The child's problem suddenly becomes to suppress that smile and being able to hold back even the shadow of her interior giggles. Go with the roll. Shrink down to the child's world.

No matter how appropriately a parent corrects the child's false views, the other parent and her lawyer can be guaranteed to complain to the court with exaggerated gusto. Expect it. This is one fight you can't avoid. Trying to avoid it runs the real risk that the other parent will succeed in their goal and permanently fracture the bond between you and your children. There is no higher sin for the courts to commit than to rob a child of their father and the child from the father.

Being a party to parental alienation is child abuse, pure and simple.

This is another situation requiring fathers to be careful with language. Your child knows very well something major is happening but they can't figure out why they have less time with you. Even if you believe mom is the reason, you must never say so. Never blame the mother. At times this seems impossible, particularly if your child is full of questions, and can easily tell that you believe you are feeding them false information. Do your best to get around or avoid the subject. To the question "Why can't I stay for one more night," you should reply, "Your mother and I are working on it." It is damned difficult to withhold the logical response: "Ask your mom." Don't do that. You ask it of the mother's lawyer once a week.

Talk to your child about how you can't really talk to them frankly about it. Let them you understand their confusion and hurt. Comfort them with the assurance things will improve. Hold them tight. If you didn't cuddle or hug your kids much before, you should draw your kids into it now. They need it.

CHAPTER 24: WHAT JUDGES DO AND DON'T WANT TO SEE

Judges don't want to see or hear you do any of these things:

- Badmouth the mother.
- Send the monthly support check with the child.
- Frequently are not on time for pick up or drop off the child with the mother.
- Discuss the case with your child.
- Take up with another woman (or women) to the knowledge of the children too soon after the separation.

There is no better anti-depressant for a recently separated man than a new woman. For a recently separated father the need for a fix of substitute love and affection can be overpowering. Resist. There are good reasons for this. Firstly, this type of documented "re-bounding" can quickly become addictive and used as a false and momentary high to smother pain. Pain must be fully felt and acknowledged to ever be overcome. Dulling it with alcohol, work, or women is a short term fix that you must not permit to become habitual. There is nothing you can do about it. Accept it. Live it. Most importantly, learn from it.

The second reason directly affects your children. Children of separated parents can feel responsibility for the break-up. They fear the loss of love from one or both parents. If you are seen by your child too suddenly with another woman, it will serve to verify in your child's mind that your love is going elsewhere and they may feel abandoned.

This is not to say that after an appropriate amount of time, when the children have stabilized in their new life, you can't start dating. But even then the children must remain your first priority, and a new girlfriend be made to understand. If she doesn't understand this, or is negative to the children's mother, or thinks she is a replacement mother – stop seeing her. Fast. There are a lot of fine women looking for the kind of man you are capable of being. You are in transition. She will should agree to wait for the man you will become.

Patience is the name of the game. No matter how fantastic she may be in every other department, if your current girlfriend isn't right for your kids, let her go.

It is extremely important that your children not even know about the existence of a new girlfriend until you have reached the point where you both see a continuing and serious relationship. Then the children can be gradually brought into the picture.

It goes without saying that there should be no overnight stay at your home that the children can learn about until you feel there is a solid foundation for a continuing relationship.

Be prepared for the ex to escalate the conflict when she hears you have another woman in your life. It is amazing how predictable mothers react this way. This is a third reason to not have a new relationship until divorce is behind you.

When I was young my parents divorced. A few years later my father took me and my sister to dinner in New York with the woman he wanted to marry. In the cab he took the occasion to explain the kind of love he had for the woman he intended to marry. She was someone we had come to know and like. He told us his love for her had grown new in his heart. It was not part of the love he had for us. It developed out of a different part of his heart. The love he had for us was all still there.

Judges don't want to see or hear of fathers that:

- Withhold child support because of something the mother has or hasn't done.

When the mother does something she clearly shouldn't, or violates an existing court order, a frequent and initially natural knee-jerk response by the father is retaliation. This thinking, if acted upon, will always lead to trouble. The first task is to recognize a knee-jerk reaction for what it is. Next, practice reacting to it in a way that allows you to vent your negative emotion without it becoming part of the dispute. Ultimately, the goal is to not react at all to her continuing poor behavior. You could be in for years of it.

A common knee-jerk response is to hold back financial payments. Refusing to pay child support, for instance. This is completely counter-productive. No matter how bizarre the behavior of the mother, how much money she is ripping you off for, there is never an excuse to hold back child support – court-ordered or not. If you think the issue is big enough to warrant a change in the child support order, bring a court application.

In the collection of wrong moves that can come back and bite you in the ass big time in court, withholding child support for whatever reason is the granddaddy of them all.

What A Judge Does Want To See In You
Judges do want to hear that you:

- Will go the extra mile.
- Have found an apartment or house in the same school catchment area as the mother to be nearer his children.
- Have taken or are taking post-separation parenting courses.
- Has taken or will take communication counseling with his ex.
- Has gotten over the "blame" issues.
- Has a reasoned and workable parenting plan and schedule for how he will parent and maintain the children, including details of the home, food, sleep, activities, family connections, etc.
- Is totally familiar with the child's school, teacher and principal and any health care professionals.

- Fosters the children's connections with their mother, grandparents, and extended family on both sides equitably.
- Doesn't count every minute to make a case for time with the children.

Let me explain each item individually:

- Will go the extra mile.

There is a large basket of ideas on how to accomplish "extra effort." Obviously restraint by you in circumstances that are trying is one. Doing things for your children – and for the mother – above and beyond what is ordered or expected is also going the extra mile. Keeping the mother on medical benefits with your employer when you don't have to is going the extra mile. As is taking an anger management course voluntarily when you aren't angry, but she says you are. When she asks for extra time to take the children to something they will enjoy, let her do it once in a while. Don't demand make up time unless you have very little to start with.

- Have found an apartment or house in the same school catchment area as the mother to be nearer his children.

- Have taken or are taking post-separation parenting courses.

You may know more about what it takes to be a good parent than the mother. Unless you have previously raised children as a single parent. you should still take any available courses. Some jurisdictions mandate it. Take as many as you can. Load up on good books to read.

- Has taken or will take communication counseling with his ex.

Many mothers claim they can't communicate with ex-spouses. In the past, this was a surefire way of getting awarded sole custody. It is no longer that easy. But too many mothers still adopt this tactic. Some refuse to talk or e-mail or fax. That actually is a failure to communicate – their failure. More often than not what is meant when a mother tells a court or swears in an affidavit that the parties can't communicate is that they fail to agree. Separated couples can communicate through pages of faxes and hundreds of e-mails on many subjects. Simple failure to be able to agree on the subject is not a failure to communicate.

- Has gotten over the "blame" issues.

Remember: Fix the problem, not the blame.
Getting beyond destructive emotions is a survival issue. If and when you end up in court on the witness stand, you want the judge to see that you are no longer mired in the past, still throwing the same old mud at the other side. Leave it to the other side to come into court with large rearview mirrors on each shoulder. Your focus is on the children's future. You will get the judge's positive attention.

- Has a reasoned and workable parenting plan and schedule for how he will parent and maintain the children, including details of the home, food, sleep, activities, family connections, etc.

If you are lucky enough to have a job with flexible hours, your children will benefit from more time with you. The same if you are self-employed. The judge needs hard evidence that this is the case. Present a parenting plan which demonstrates exactly how you will parent when the children are with you. Keep your ex informed of the children's schedules for baths, sleep and meals, and seek her schedules in return. Try and make them as similar as possible.

A letter from your employer supporting and approving your parenting plan is valuable. Offer to let the mother come on over and check your children's living arrangements. As stated elsewhere when you are looking to find a place for yourself and your children, it is great to let the kids play a big role in picking out your home including their rooms, the color of paint for their rooms, etc. This gives them a real sense of belonging and empowerment.

- Is totally familiar with the child's school, teacher and principal and any health care professionals.

It is not uncommon in an intact marriage for one parent to do the majority, if not all, the arrangements for doctor's and dentist's appointments. This is part of the agreed-upon division of responsibility within the marriage. Often only one parent stays in touch with the school teachers and attends meetings with teachers.

If you had little to do with health care providers or teachers during the marriage it is important you go out of your way to catch up on this. If there are after-school coaches, get on a first-name basis with them also. You can expect to receive sarcastic comments from the mother to the effect that "you never were concerned or involved with these sorts of child-related matters in the past." Your sudden interest is suspect. Or that you are trying to win "dad of the year" award or some such nonsense. That's par for the course with some mothers. Most judges don't buy this attitude. When hearing such an argument from a disgruntled mother an ironic judge may reply, "Well, aren't you glad he is now so concerned?"

- Fosters the children's connections with their mother, grandparents, and extended family on both sides equitably.

In our culture when we talk about the love and nurture a child requires for healthy emotional development, we envisage a biological mother and father. Other cultures more easily recognize children's need for love and nurture, and it matters less who they get it from as long as they get it. The fortunate children in our society are those who have involved extended family members. This is good for all children. During the marriage break-up these aunts, uncles and grandparents become particularly important. It is obviously very important for both parents to put in the extra effort to keep these relationships active for the children. A key warning sign that your ex is attempting to alienate the children against you is if she denies a meaningful relationship between your children and your family. Your family members should be encouraged to maintain contact with you ex and her family. If they don't see much of your children on your limited time they should attempt to get their own independent time with the children.

Of course, the odds are if your reading this book your ex is doing her best to move her whole family side away from you and your family.

- Doesn't count every minute to make a case for time with the children.

Judges look to see which parent is less hung up on the strict terms of an access order and will give the other parent some special time without always demanding make-up time. Naturally, if you are consistently losing important time with your children and it becomes a regular event, stop it. That is a different story. But for special occasions, if the children will enjoy doing what the mother is requesting special time for, go for it. And if she thinks she has pulled one over on you by getting extra time without having to give you make up time, so what? Leave her with that thought. Your focus should be whether the children have a good always time. You gave it to them just as much as she did.

A former client once had a break-through experience with his ex who, five years after the divorce, remained totally obsessed with continuing the "fight." She had an almost pathological need to be seen as the better parent. Everything dad did with their child, she had to do better. Dad wanted to switch a weekend so he could take their daughter to Ice Capes. The mother then scooped him by buying tickets the same day and told him "no" she would take the girl. For her parenting was a blood sport. She always had to be right and always denied him what he might want. One long weekend, there was a choice about whether the child was to be parented by the mother on a Thursday or a Friday. My friend wanted Friday as his parenting time. So he let it slip ever so subtly that if it was no real matter to her, he would prefer the Thursday. Quick as a mousetrap snaps, she triumphantly claimed Thursday for herself. My client was delighted because he had long ago detached from her and it didn't bother him at all that she might think she was winning every hand. He got his Friday.

The good news for this great dad is that his daughter, when she got into college, she came to realize he actually was a very good father, and not at all the bad guy her mother had portrayed him as over the intervening years.

It is my experience that in heavily contested custody disputes, where one or both parents grill the children or badmouth the other parent, the children just want to escape the situation. If one parent grills them upon the return from the other parent, and the other parent doesn't, and one parent badmouths the other parent but the other parent doesn't, the child will slowly gravitate toward the proper parent. This is because they feel they are in a demilitarized zone with the proper parent. They will grow to appreciate the parent who leaves them in peace.

There are subtle distinctions between proper and improper inquiries to make of a child upon returning from their other home. Instead of a question, "What did you do with your mother?" – which might put the child on the spot, make a statement instead such as, "I hope you had a good time with your mom. What would you like to do now?"

Keep pictures of their mother in their room at your house. Regardless of how you may personally feel about the woman, make positive comments about her to the children. Make sure the children know that you know how important she is to them.

If questioned by a court appointed evaluator the child can honestly speak of your values.

Take advantage of the time when the children are with their mother to rededicate yourself, to refocus, plan and just generally learn the hard task of being happy and content in their absence. Update your journal where you keep a complete record of everything involving the children. (Caution: because your journal may be produced to the other side or for court, bear in mind that everything you write may be seen by a judge. Apply the general rules being discussed here in your journal. In many jurisdictions a journal kept for the purposes of court preparation is privileged and can't be forcibly produced by the other side.) Work on developing your new life. Reconnect with the friends who may have been left by the wayside of your separation. Make new friends, particularly single dads and moms. Time spent away from your children should be dedicated to working on yourself.

If you have a court trial looming in your future, you want to be able to call as witnesses parents who see you with your kids. You should be consciously seeking out friendships with such neighbors, especially mothers.

It is important that while the children are with their mother, you make the time to touch base with the teachers and administrators at school. And their extra-curricular activities coaches. If your kids have any medical problems, take this time on a regular basis to meet with these health care providers. This is important for two reasons: it is important you know each other and can communicate well. This is good for your children. Secondly, if the mother is inclined to create difficulties, such as spreading falsehoods, etc., these people need to know your sincerity. You never know when you may find yourself back in court defending an allegation as benign as "he doesn't care about their schooling" or as damning as "he is abusive to the child." It goes without saying that you have to be very calm and diplomatic at all times with these third parties. Never vent your negative emotions about the mother to third parties, even your family. Their opinions of your emotional state may come up in court.

Make sure the school and doctors have copies of recent court orders. Insist you be regularly provided with the information the law says you are entitled to. If the mother has falsely raised issues with the police in the past, inform the local detachment where you live and how they can get a hold of you if they need to. Give the police copies of any court orders. Let the mother know you have done this. It might give her pause before acting inappropriately again.

Today's technology will permit you to set up e-mail accounts and video hook-ups with your children at their mother's home. Find the children interesting and safe places to visit on the Internet. Learn from them. Play games and interact with them. If the mother resists, obtain a court order to permit you to organize this. Let the kids be involved in planning what they will do when they see you next.

As children get older, they benefit from increasing time away from both parents. It is obviously very hard for an "every other weekend" father to volunteer up valuable time for the kids to be away from him with other kids, or at sporting events. Do your best.

One of the most common abuses of the system that too many mothers pull is setting the kids up in so many after-school activities that there is less and less time for the father. It is tactic #1 in the play book of personality disordered mothers. The only time the father sees the kids is driving them to and from pre-planned events and putting them to bed four times a month. The valid idea that children need after-school and weekend activities is all too easily abused by a mother who schedules these events on the father's parenting time. If you want to do something to correct this abuse, do it sooner rather than later. Once such a restrictive schedule is in place it is difficult to change.

Finally, some comment on the futility and counterproductive effort of trying to reason with your ex via faxes or e-mails. Like the cancer specialist who only sees very sick people, trial lawyers in divorce court see only the worst marriage breakdowns. As a lawyer who represents primarily, but not exclusively, fathers, I find the mothers on the opposite side of these highly conflicted files are tragic individuals. A significant majority have horrific unresolved childhood issues. These issues cause them to need their children to be emotional crutches for their unmet needs, issues that morph into weapons used against the father. These unmet needs propel some mothers to trial, failing at all attempts at negotiation or mediation. They will never – can never – voluntarily give up control. The these women were tragically abused or abandoned in their childhood. Others had parents that exerted a very unhealthy control over their lives. Frequently these mothers suffer from one or more personality disorders. In other words, they are ill and need to be seen and treated with compassion.

There is something about men that makes us blind to these sides of women with whom we fall in love. Then when we start to see their darker side, rather than retreat, we convince ourselves we are knights on a white horse that can rescue her from her demons. Even where no parent, friend or other male partner has been able to provide meaningful help. How quickly we can become co-dependent with such needy women. And some of us, even after the marriage is clearly over, continue to play this role – hoping that for the good of the children, they will see the light, mend their ways, and everyone's problems will all be over. Unfortunately, this can be dangerous wishful thinking. History disputes it.

Too many of my clients show me a history of faxes or e-mails sent to the mother full of these pleadings for rationality, fairness and common sense. I have a theory that a great many of the mothers I deal with on the other sides of my files get a sick satisfaction from receiving these kinds of communications. These pleas for understanding simply add more fuel to her determination to wage war. She gains needed satisfaction in knowing that she still has the power to make him come pleading. This constant engagement in the fight soon becomes her self-definition. "I'm the person whose job it is to save my children from him!" They become obsessed and dedicated to conflict as a life's work.

Their lawyers spout "For the sake of the children." Gimme a break.

The sooner you learn to restrict your communications to a statement of simple facts, the sooner you will emotionally detach from the mother. Detaching from her is the single most important first step in your own recovery. The grieving process does not quickly pass. Don't be surprised at how hard it is to accomplish. It certainly would be great if she went into serious psychotherapy and got better, for her sake and your children's. But there is nothing you can do now to make that happen. Having said that, if she so clearly has psychopathology that could be proven in court – always hard to do unless child services has had to step in and you have good medical expert evidence – then the court might take notice. Otherwise, all you can do is help your children as best you can.

A Court Room is Not the Place to Prove Your Moral Superiority

When one or both parents fail to resolve their case and end up before a judge, they nearly always have at least two agendas: One, the only one capable of implementation, is to win for the children fair time with both parents or deny the children fair time with the other parent. The second agenda is to finally have a stage upon which their story of unjust, unethical and mean treatment by the other spouse can finally be told. Every person's day in court. Each hopes that a judge will side with them and against the other parent. They expect the judge to condemn the other parent in words so strong and clear that their own vindication is won. Parents with strong religious convictions typically have these expectations. Such expectations are misplaced and dangerous. While it may have been the case many decades ago, family law is no longer a morality play. A courtroom is not the Pearly Gates where you get the chance to convince St Peter he should welcome you with open arms and kick the ex straight to hell. If you believe in Heaven and Hell you will have to wait until you are called.

Judges want to hear only what will help them determine

the short-term future of the children. They know the parents have separated. They could care less why or how the parents separated. They certainly don't want to hear that one or both parents is still carrying such a grudge that the separation battle still exists. But that is exactly what is happening in so many of the high conflict cases. The parent who tries to drag their personal fight into the courtroom will be less appreciated, particularly if it is the father. Unfortunately, for reasons of residues of bias, naiveté, and failing to recognize mental illness, judges get too easily hood winked by some of these mothers.

On occasion family members on both sides take the witness stand and vent negativity toward the other family. Again, that is not what the court wants to hear. Don't do it!

It is not good enough that you artificially take this advice, then begrudgingly get up on the witness stand and fake it. If your ex's lawyer is a good cross-examiner it will be easy for them to get your simmering negativity into the open. You are merely a pawn in the courtroom where that lawyer makes his or her living. It is very easy for him or her to expose your animosities if you have not sincerely overcome them. The message is clear: Do whatever it takes to come to grips with your issues and do whatever work is required to overcome shortcomings. That way you will be seen as honest and sincere on the witness stand. Truth is your   sword   and   shield.

CHAPTER 25: RATIONAL VS MORAL WAR

"War is a continuation of politics by other means."

— Carl von Clausewitz.

Litigation and courtroom tactics are frequently talked about with analogies to war. I am purposefully guilty of that in this book. One can argue that litigation is a continuation by one parent of the need to control by other means. To a father fighting for his children, the metaphor is apt.

In the 20th century, nation states adopted laws and conventions aimed at limiting the right of states to war with each other. One of the historical justifications the modern realist theorists sought to remove was the so-called "just" war. War needed to be narrowed to rational situations. The imperial powers, to keep their control of the world, needed to remove religion as a justification for war. Other people's morality couldn't be permitted to interfere with their ruling of the world. In the late 20th century that attempt collapsed. "Human rights" became the new "just war." Morality was back in the saddle. The chaos this brings is obvious to anyone who follows today's world events.

There is an analogy to be drawn here with the conflict between separating couples. In general terms – there are always exceptions – men who work in business try to bring that rationality to their home lives. Courts like rationality. If there is to be an argument or a legal fight, such argument should be limited to matters capable of being presented rationally by the imposition of logic and common sense.

In very simple terms, we can say that most men, when dealing with the outside world, typically prefer to play by sets of rationally understood and accepted rules. In similarly simplistic and exaggerated terms we can say that most women play more by subjective rules. By this is meant that they are often more motivated by intuition and emotion. Evolution produced this difference for the survival of the species.

Any theory of argument that allows for different and often opposing perspectives and judgments is a rational approach to problem solving. Where one refuses to listen to or entertain another's reasons, arguments premised on the authority of morality often come into play. A mother – or father – who fights on and on in court without rational reason, claiming an intuitive knowledge of what "is right" for their children, is waging war on the basis of morality – a just war. Just wars do not lend themselves to logic. They are fueled by faith. Once the mother starts, she cannot accept that there are other valid sides to the issue because to do so is to admit defeat. Men are not immune from acting on faith and belief.

A rational parent, mother or father, who find themselves caught in this cyclone of emotion and irrationality have few skills to combat it. They need to extract themselves physically and emotionally from the battle field. Or they are going to go to trial. No interim steps along the way are going to miraculously witness logic and rational reasoning conquer blind faith.

I have seen too many good and decent fathers fail to recognize the extent of irrationality governing the beliefs and actions of the mother. In some ways it is understandable. Unlike people in the mental health professions, or experienced family lawyers, the average husband/father may not have had any previous experience with a personality disordered close friend or loved one. They may too quickly pass off the occasional display of odd behavior as just something to learn to live with, like a mole on your lover's cheek.

Whereas that same display of odd behavior, to the mind of a mental health expert, would be recognized as a symptom of an underlying mental condition. The practical result is that most men in this situation remain naively blind to the reality of their situation. They persist in thinking they are dealing with a mentally healthy adult. They are forever pleading with the woman to "please see what you are doing to our child!" They don't realize that every reasonable request made for the benefit of the child just fuels these tragic mothers in their campaign.

On the flip side, there are fathers who think that because the mother seems to exhibit bi polar or borderline personality traits, and a hate on for the father, she should by definition be deemed unfit and he should be the primary parent. Ah, if only it were that simple. The question is how far from the socially acceptable norm should any parent have to stray to trigger intervention by the state or the court?

In my experience the majority of fathers dealing with mildly disordered mothers recognize the vital importance of that woman in the life of their child. These men seek equal time shared parenting. The exception of course is where the disorder is adversely affecting the child. That is a different fact   pattern   entirely.

CHAPTER 26: COURT FALLACIES AND MYTHS

The discredited myths of the maternal preference and the tender years doctrine are alive and well in the fallacy of the so called "primary parent." The designation "primary parent" as having any relevant meaning requires judicial euthanasia as soon as possible. Usually it doesn't mean a thing.

The rules of evidence stand apart in family court with its often uncritical acceptance of false conclusions from untrue propositions introduced under the guise of evidence. Prime among these is the fallacy of the primary parent.

If a lawyer from another universe were to sit in family chambers long enough, he/she/it would hear lawyers claiming for their mother client they were the primary parent. The lawyer would spread out their open palms and ask for the children to be granted to their mother client by fiat. Magically, the judge would comply. After witnessing many of these successful applications by primary parents, the stranger would be consumed by one overpowering thought: Why did no judge ever require the primary parent's lawyer to prove by expert evidence that being the so-called primary parent had any long-term benefit to a child that the so-called secondary parent could not provide? Judges are supposed to be gate keepers stopping unverifiable propositions from escaping into acceptance. Therefore, as in other areas of the law, the stranger naturally assumed that there must be a leading case somewhere establishing that children do better under primary than secondary parents. One perhaps from a Court of Appeal that established that a primary parent was, by all the best pedagogical research, the better parent for the child. Having been proven by expert evidence in some great trial, it required no further effort or expense to prove it in each chambers application or trial.

A thorough research would uncover no such case. There

is no such evidence. Never has been. No lawyer pleading his/her case on behalf of a so-called primary parent as ever been put to the task of proving just exactly what that means other a string of nouns proving nothing. Yet still today, judges seem to accept as judicial notice that the primary parent is the default parent. It is an extraordinary failure on the part of the court. No judge would wear a similar blinder in a medical malpractice or personal injury trial. It is antithetical to the best interest of the child.

A father of a young child enlists and goes off to war for 10 months. He returns. No one suggests that his child can't be parented by him on the exact same basis when the father initially left. Yet every minute of every hour of every court day mother enabling lawyers fight to prevent fathers seeing their children after only a couple of months of absence.

Double standards are the floor tile of some family courts.

CHAPTER 27: PASSION IN COURT

"The unthinking respect for authority is
the greatest enemy of truth." — Albert
Einstein

A courtroom can seem a strange and alien place even for a visitor. It can be slightly terrifying to an unrepresented father starting out. This applies to interim or simple hearings in motions court as well as to the eventual trial itself. It is mandatory that you spend time observing various court proceedings. They are open to the public. Inquire at the registry in the court where you expect to have to appear. Ask for the names and room numbers of hotly contested family cases. Prepare to be patient and sit through not very interesting or exciting stuff. It will not be like a TV show. Watch and learn all that you can. Try and take in the cross examination of one parent by opposing counsel. That is where you can learn the most.

Check out the demeanor and mannerism of different witnesses. Visualize how you might best be your own witness when it comes to be your turn. Sense how you would be serious and matter of fact when required. Importantly, never stifle appropriate emotion. When it comes to argument feel free to demonstrate passion for what you seek and for your family. Don't overdo it. There is a fine line to be drawn there.

You will find, as all witnesses do, that after a few minutes in the witness stand the anxieties and fears subside.

When you are giving your own evidence from notes or memory or spontaneously, speak and look to the judge. When being cross examined by opposing counsel, answer back to the lawyer. Engage the lawyer with your eyes. If you are too shy, the lawyer might ratchet up his tempo to take advantage of you. If you are too aggressive back, you may only start a verbal fight you can't win. Just be yourself.

Polite. A humble but proud father. Find the middle ground of civil discourse. If you find the lawyer coming on hard, just hold your ground. Cross examination is the firing range. Lawyers are allowed to dig for what they seek. A good judge will know when and how to tell such a lawyer to back off. No matter how hard the attack – which it very rarely is – take the hardest hits, the worst false allegations, on the chest and keep hold of appropriate emotion.

Having said that I need to expunge images of fierce lawyers looking like wolves. In family cases, when a lawyer does that it is an admission that they have lost not only control of the case, but of themselves. The ones to watch carefully are the quiet, methodical types. Never lose your cool.

CHAPTER 28: TAKE A POLYGRAPH

Polygraph (otherwise known as a lie detector) test results are allowed into evidence in some jurisdictions and not in others. Regardless as to the rule in your jurisdiction, you should definitely give very serious consideration to taking the test as long as it's administered by a recognized expert in the field.

There are two reasons for this. If your jurisdiction allows the introduction of the test result into evidence (i.e. the opinion of an expert that you not only passed the test but the expert believes you were truthful) then you will have some compelling evidence to support your denial.

If your jurisdiction does not allow you to introduce the result through a qualified expert, you can at the very least put into evidence the fact that you took the test and passed it. Reporting that you passed a polygraph is certainly better than not being able to say anything. No matter how loud opposing counsel objects, the trial judge knows you had the inner conviction of truth to even take the test.

To be clear: there is a significant difference between you testifying that you took and passed a test, and being able to file an expert opinion report as to the significance of the results. An analogy would be you testifying that you got rear ended in a car accident and your neck has been hurting ever since. That is of limited value. An expert opinion medical report from a neck specialist explaining the muscle tear and the strain on your vertebra and the degree of actual impairment would be ever so much more significant to a judge.

You should meet and talk with a polygraph expert. You should explain all the circumstances around the allegation you are trying to refute. That person should explain everything to you. You should also be given the questions that would be asked. Only if you feel confident of passing should you proceed.

To maximize the strength of the test, you should seriously consider advising the opposing party before taking the test of your intention to do so. This will strengthen your integrity, especially in a jurisdiction that does not allow the admission of the result. The mere fact that you were confident enough to announce in advance of your intention, and that you then went and took the test, and most important that you have provided the other side with the result, will help persuade the judge of your credibility. Be certain to point out to the judge that if you had failed the test the other side would be making a big deal of it.

A person solid in their knowledge that they are truthful, but quite anxious over the idea of taking a polygraph test, has been known to not tell anyone in advance of an intention to take the test, but takes the test. Where they fail they don't tell anyone. If they pass, they have then advised opposing counsel of an intention to take the test, and go to another polygrapher and repeat the test.

You may have opportunities to give the good polygraph test results to agencies that historically put weight on such tests, such as child welfare agencies and the police. If a psychologist is doing a parenting capacity investigation get a copy to that person.

CHAPTER 29:   MINING THE OPPOSITION

The function of spies during warfare is to uncover the battle plans of the opposition. There is no equivalent person in family law litigation. Your best source of intel on the other side comes from the mother of your children and her lawyer. The more helpless and dumb and out of your depth they think you are, and the more arrogant and self-righteous they are, the more useful information you can usually mine from them.

As you know from your own experience, it is human nature for separating partners, and their lawyers, to try and intimidate the other with the overpowering ethical righteousness of their arguments and positions. You, in your turn, just like a lawyer, muster up your best argument in support of your position and fling it right back. Each side struggles for the higher moral ground in the belief that reason and logic will prevail and the other side will back down or concede.

You are badly mistaken if you think reason and common sense will ever prevail over the other side. As explained in this book, mothers needing to maintain control are awash with psychological and emotional contradictions. Reason plays second fiddle. Self-serving platitudes and rationalizations will be cloaked as reasonable arguments.

An experienced lawyer will regard the facts of their client's case as chess pieces, or limited rounds of ammunition, each to be used sparingly and for a specific purpose. If the case goes nuclear and ends up in a trial, that lawyer wants to have kept some big ammo in reserve. That means there are some facts that the lawyer does their best to keep from the other side. It takes years in the gauntlet of court room trials to know what to use early on, to maximize the prospects of settlement, and what to hold in reserve for the trial.

It is often difficult – and depending upon the rules of

disclosure in your jurisdiction nearly impossible – to hide documents and witnesses from the other side. But tactics, and types of arguments, and the "spin" you are going to put on something, all of these can be kept private and not disclosed. It is these latter parts of your case that you risk losing in the animated verbal discussions with your former partner's lawyer or her. It is these important arrows in your quiver or tools in your toolbox that you want to keep private and not disclose. As well as any facts and documents that you can, without risking not being able to use them at trial for failure to properly disclose earlier on.

Some discussion between the lawyers and or the parties is obviously useful. Rational parties and adept legal negotiators can often resolve disputes in that fashion. It is doubtful, however, if your situation has led you to read this or other such books, that such rationality exists on the other side.

In high conflict cases, I will often provoke a lawyer, who hasn't already opened up, to "argue" his or her case with me on the phone or outside the courtroom. Or in e-mails or letters. I will respond with just enough feigned indignation or concern to keep the lawyer feeding me their views on everything and how they intend to prove it all. Occasionally, if I see an appropriate opening, I will use a big piece from my arsenal of facts, when to do so has a reasonable chance of winning the point. But that too takes years of practice to recognize that particular moment.

The hardest temptation to resist is when you are in a mediation type process and you feel she and/or her lawyer are winning the day. Your very being shakes with conviction that if you just let out your reserve ammunition, you could sway the mediator and your ex. Never forget this: mediation fails miserably with mothers who have their own agenda, are alienators, or are personality disordered. Unless the court rules mandate mediation, save your money and stay away from it. Often the mediator will be a judge. The same rule applies. You have to get used to judges, and mediators, and opposing lawyers, thinking like she does, that somehow you are being non-cooperative and not serious about resolving the matter, that you are intent to fight to the bitter end for what you want, being blind to the needs of the children. They are right. You are prepared to stick to your guns, come hell or high water.

You will discover early on that the more pig headed you are perceived to be by the other side, the higher up they will ratchet their attack and the more gems they will give you to help you prepare for the inevitable trial.

You can expect the mother to tell the children it is all your fault that the family is still in a big legal fight. Your option is to head her off at the pass. Get to the kids first. Give them a simple, non-blaming, short explanation to the effect that you and their mother are continuing to try and work things out with the help of a judge. And leave it at that. If they come back with, "Well mommy says it is all your fault!", sit them down and tell them most things in life are not simple. Most things are complicated. Don't tell them that mommy is wrong. Just that the two of your see things differently. With the passage of time, they will grow to understand which parent tried best to establish a demilitarized   zone.

CHAPTER 30: POSSESSIONS & THE NEW APARTMENT

Where you have to leave the matrimonial home and find a new place to live, and circumstances permit, locate two or three possible new apartments in the same school catchment area. Then let your children decide which one they like best. Let them pick their bedrooms. Let them choose the color of fresh paint if required in their new bedroom. This should help lessen the separation anxiety and give the children a sense of ownership of the new home with you. This in turn is a shield against a mother intent on disparaging and demeaning you to the children.

If it works, have pets. Tropical fish, guinea pig or a dog. Beware the pet competition game.

Possessions

We have all been raised in a consumer society that has conditioned us to want more and more material possessions. The notion that physical possessions can be a primary source of happiness is wrong. We have been conditioned that we are not really all we can or should be without lots of toys.

In divorce, each party has to give up things, a radical reversal of the cycle of collecting. You must learn to detach and not fight. Of course, house and money are important. But neither is as important as your own happiness. If you see or define your happiness as involving house and money, then you really do have a problem.

This is a perfect area to practice non-attachment.

CHAPTER 31: MOVING OUT

A good time to negotiate a reasonable parenting schedule is before you move out of the matrimonial home when your ex is demanding it. Her wanting you out is a good bargaining chip – maybe your only one. You can agree to find your own place provided there is a reasonable parenting agreement put in place, in writing. Make the best of it. Be patient. Be humble.

Most couples upon separation have to sell the matrimonial home. Neither one has the financial strength to buy the other's interest. Children have a natural attachment to their home with both parents. The parent who can remain in the family home has an advantage with the children's unconscious preferences on where they want to live.

Mothers intuit this more than fathers. Fear of losing this advantage causes mothers to escalate the drama in the hope you will over react and they can call the police. If that doesn't work, some run off with the kids to a women's shelter with a manufactured tale of domestic abuse.

If you are still living in the matrimonial home with your spouse, you have a unique opportunity. Gather up some money and go talk with an experienced family lawyer. Ask him/her about the rules and laws that govern in your jurisdiction. Ask any questions arising out reading this or other self-help books.

CHAPTER 32:   SUPPORT CHECKS

Don't send the mother child support checks with the kids. When lawyers for mothers have nothing of substance to argue about, they love to be super critical of a dad who "gets the child involved" by putting a cheque for mom in the four-year-old's knapsack.

There is absolutely nothing wrong with dad telling mom at the beginning of the month "Oh by the way your cheque is in the diaper bag" or "in the knapsack." As in so many areas of parenting, there comes a time when a child's age may make it inappropriate to send the cheque in that fashion. Play it safe. Don't put the money in the diaper bag unless the mother is on written record as being okay with that. Even if the mother says it's okay or even asks you to please put the checks in the kids' bag, get it confirmed in writing or an e-mail if you have any fear of future argument. It may seem completely innocent and obviously the best thing to do – at the moment. Right. That's what you thought when you married her.

The point being that you should not voluntarily put yourself in a situation that if it backfired might hurt you.

CHAPTER 33:   SET MONEY ASIDE

Good parents place their relationship with their children as the most important goal in their life. Money matters, physical assets, property, and investments may be secondary but they are always critically important. This book has not the space to adequately address financial issues. However, as you prepare to represent yourself in court, it is important to marshal some assets to cover required costs even if you aren't paying a lawyer.

Once litigation is commenced courts have rules requiring full disclosure by both parents to the other of their financial assets, income and debts.   There are applications that can be brought by the lawyer for the mother asking a judge to freeze assets and savings in your name. You will be left able to access your money to meet normal loving expenses. If there are limited funds to begin with it is important to put some aside for court purposes. These funds may be required to retain a court-appointed expert to evaluate both parents and the children, and ultimately make recommendations to the court. You may want to hire your own expert for some purpose. Sooner rather than later, you should consider getting sufficient funds out of accounts that might soon become subject to freeze or restraining orders. You can transfer funds to a parent or friend.

Keep in mind at all times that your financial records – bank and credit card statements – are producible. How you spend your money and where you put it cannot be kept secret. If you do transfer funds, be certain to fully detail what you are doing in the bank records. You don't want to be accused to trying to hide money. If the funds you transfer are family assets, to which you ex has a claim, you may want to only take half the funds available to transfer to a family member or friend. Let her have the other half.

One exception to what has just been written above is where you may be on the hook to pay debts or credit cards for items used by both of you or just her before the separation. Or maybe she has to pay a debt of yours in which case you will owe her something. If this applies to you, determine the mounts before removing funds form any account.

If there is matrimonial home in one or both of your names with monthly mortgage payments to be made, insure funds remain available to meet that debt.

If your ex has a variety of bank accounts and various valuable assets, be proactive and apply before a judge to get an order preventing her from disposing of any of her assets.

Find out how to put a lien or charge on the matrimonial home or any property in her name to prevent sale or mortgaging to give her money to fight you.

CHAPTER 34:   PEACE BONDS

A common tactic by a mother seeking to unfairly win custody of their child is to falsely accuse the father of abuse or assault, or precipitate an incident and call the police. The police arrive and arrest the father. The father spends some time in jail. A lawyer gets him out. The lawyer talks to the prosecutor. The prosecutor offers a deal. The lawyer advises the father to sign a peace bond and your criminal charge will be dropped. The father feels a rush of relief and agrees to sign and leaves the court house. Bad move. A really bad move.

If this happens to you, don't sign the peace bond or agree to a restraining order that isn't mutual. In the hands of the mother's lawyer, your signature on a peace bond is second best to a conviction. Your signature can come back to haunt you. Your criminal lawyer may be good at what he/she does, and in other circumstances his/her advice might be worth taking. But not for a falsely accused father. Unless there is evidence sufficient to convict you, you should take it to trial.

If agreeing to a peace bond is your best way out, insure that the wording does not prevent you from communicating with or about your children.

If this happens to you try and retain a criminal lawyer who has had experience in or understands family law custody disputes. In any metropolitan area there are many criminal lawyers familiar with peace bonds coming out of false allegations of abuse.

CHAPTER 35: VISITATION AND FOLLOWING ORDERS

The classic stories in every culture tell us that humans learn life's hardest lessons when times are hardest, when we are so far down we have lost hope of ever getting up again. It is at those moments a man finds out what sort of inner strength he is made of. All good stories have a "dark night of the soul" when we descend into the dark ashes of doom. Don't be discouraged when you're feeling all is lost.

One of the most difficult moments you'll face after a separation is dropping off your child to the mother's home, saying goodbye in awkward circumstances. The drive home is one of the loneliest moments you'll have to endure. It might be another two weeks before you get to see your child again. Irrational fears jump across your mind, especially if the child is really young: will my kid even remember me?

Jealously wells up against the child's mother when she has a near monopoly on being with and caring for the child. This brings back to the surface all the despair, anger, and hurt from the last stages of the marriage. Concerns about what she might say to prejudice the child against you. This injustice is all sanctioned by the courts that, up until now, you likely believed represented fairness and justice. That myth is shattered.

No matter what your situation, following the conditions of your access and visitation court order are extremely important. You violate them at your peril. Even if the kids seem to like you less and less every time you drop them off and pick them up again, or even if they start to beg you more and more not to take them back to their mother, you must abide by court orders.

Each divorce is unique. The individuals involved and your situation may range from having the mother grant you extra time because she wants a babysitter to having her plan trips out of town or activities for the kids that interfere with every scheduled visit. The important thing to remember when you encounter problems with parenting time or struggle with compliance is that mistakes you make now, when in an emotional state, may haunt you in court. Judges want you to respect the orders of other judges. Even when those orders are not, or cause you pain.

It's hard to deal with your own loss and sadness when your time with your children is limited. This is made even tougher if your child, living primarily with their mother, starts asking for more time to live with his father, or even starts talking about "running away" from mom's home. Running away can mean anything from refusing to go home after school to walking to a friend's house, calling a relative, taking a bus to dad's home or, if sufficiently desperate, actually sneaking away and hiding somewhere.

No matter how weakly or strongly the child persists in expressing their intention; it should never be lightly regarded by parents, family members, or school personnel. The mother might construe this problem as something you have purposely designed. If it is the honestly held feeling and desire of the child to live with the father, the mother's disbelief or displeasure may result in the mother accusing the child of lying and not having the ability to know their own feelings. Aside from the insult to the child, this reaction aggravates the situation, making things worse, and increasing the risk of the child taking matters into his or her own hands. This can be very frustrating as there is little the father can do except be there to hear the child and try to explain why the court orders have to be followed, even when those orders don't make sense to the actual people having to follow them.

Children, by nature, want to help. They want their parents to feel good. They want to make their parents happy. They want to be loved. Children are very good at picking up on the subtlest of clues that a parent is sad and will want to remedy the situation. Do not make your child the only adult in your divorce. Their thoughts, their emotions, their desires, are all important for both parents to consider and important for the judge to be aware of. It is important that they feel their concerns are being addressed.

One issue in a divorce dispute will be whether or not the child is expressing independent thoughts or whether they are being encouraged to act out by a self-interested parent. Validate your child's feelings but try to help them understand that there is a process underway that may not make sense.

In some circumstances, the child might have reason to believe the mother caused the separation or is uncomfortable with the way the mother is talking about the father. It is always best for children to have two parents. Neither one can be "perfect" but that doesn't mean "unfit." If your child is asking to live with you, don't jump on that as an opportunity for advantage. The reality is that a judge will decide how this divorce ends and you should not turn your child into a shield, asking him or her to take the blows that might come at you in court. If your child wants to live with you, and is vehement, explain that you are not "the decider" but you're doing what you can to make that happen.

However, denying a child's honestly held longing for the other parent either adds determination or submerges the natural feelings down into the unconscious. This can eventually cripple the child's sense of wholeness, diminishing self-esteem, and lead to maladaptive behaviour in later life. That is why how one handles this child at this point in their life is so critical.

Non-custodial fathers of children threatening to act out have a real dilemma. They don't want to be seen as counseling the breach of a custody order. Using reason, they should do their very best to persuade the child to return to the mother every time the child asks not to have to go back. It gets more and more painful. After a while, many fathers become overwhelmed with a fear that by always making the child return to the mother they might be losing the trust of the child. They imagine the child feeling neither parent truly cares for their feelings. No child should bare that burden.

Highly conflicted or personality disordered parents are often very good at selling family, friends, teachers, counselors, lawyers, and judges the myth that the child's feelings are not their own; that they have been planted there by the other parent. Some can become very effective at pulling the wool over the eyes of others. I am talking about the hard cases. More rational parents, when met with the continuing insistence of a child who wants equal time or wants to live with the other parent, find a way to improve things. Hard cases require hard decision-making, ultimately by a judge.

Judges are more persuadable by facts and history than emotional propaganda by a parent. If Child Services have apprehended a child from a parent, or just opened a file and held an investigation over a child's threat to run, a judge will take particular notice. The credibility of the sought-for parent increases and the denial by the custodial parent often holds less weight. The more dramatic the acting out by the child, the better the chance a judge will be inclined to sanction a move to the other parent. This dynamic leads to a challenging change of approach on the part of non-custodial parent.

More often in these circumstances the custodial parent is the mother. The "dilemma" parent is more often the father. Here we are usually talking about children roughly between the ages of 8 to 12.

When patient commitment to what is expected of him only makes things worse for the child, a father's growing frustrations makes him more prepared to side with the child. At some point the father will shift from a strategy of being seen by the court as "doing the right thing", i.e. being a cop enforcing the mother's custody order, to moving a little bit out on the limb, by being there for his child.

Throughout this period of intense acting out by the child, having the child attend with a good child therapist is almost mandatory.

Your first approach should be to bring an application in court to change physical custody. If it works, great! If it doesn't, at least you have a record of the events and your attempt to resolve it within the system. If the mother will not consent to counseling for the child, ask a judge. Don't agree to a counselor who has been counselling the mother.

If none of your "within the system" efforts improve the situation for your child, you may need to push the envelope. To successfully help a child make his or her honest feelings get the significant attention they deserve, the child has to be willing to act. Some children have the inner strength to act. At the other end are children too seriously fearful of, or enmeshed with, their mother to act on their own desires. Most children range across the middle, squeezed, and stretched in both directions. Your efforts can include persistent requests of the mother, discussions with school teachers, talking to social workers, or writing a letter explaining the situation to a judge. When all else fails, acts of civil disobedience by the child may occur, such as refusal to go home with the mother from school or leaving the mother's home to go to the father's home.

Obviously, there is an enormous difference between a child who, all on their own, without any help from a parent, just suddenly ups and leaves one home for the other, and the child who has been talking about it for some time. The first could be at risk. The second can have potential risks removed by an engaged parent.

After failing within the court system, having made the decision to assist the child, the father has to sit down and carefully think of a strategy. The first consideration is to accurately gauge the inner strength of your child. How strong will he or she be when up against either the mother's tearful begging or her hurtful anger? How strong will he or she be if challenged by the police as to what he thought he was doing and why?

If there is doubt on the degree of commitment by the child, then time needs to be spent helping build up that strength.

In determining how to help strengthen and protect the child's need for self-expression, it is critical to understand the level of communications between the child and the mother. It is a very thin line between discovering if your child, by its own volition, will not tell the mother about certain things and actually asking the child to keep secrets. You don't ever want to ask the child to keep a secret from the mother. Never. It is not good for the child/mother bond present or future. It risks what doesn't need to be risked.

Some children will volunteer that when interrogated by the mother, they won't necessarily tell her some things. They have to decide on their own that they will keep some things from their mother. Primarily they won't report the discussions they are having with you about how they want to come and live with you. It can start there. But be careful because a determined mother can break a child down to report all that is being said.

Last and not least, you have to steel yourself for the guaranteed attack by the mother and her lawyer that by knowingly breaching a custody order and refusing to return the child to mother, you are exhibiting despicable behavior, are contemptuous of the court, alienating the child from the mother, and are abusive to the child by making it hold negative thoughts towards mom.

That is why it is critical that if you have early knowledge of what the child intends to do, prepare an application in court such that you can get before a judge right after the child makes its move.

The child may be forced back to the mother's primary care. It may take more than one acting out.

You may be punished by a judge. In such a case, depending on the eventual outcome, only you will know if it was worth it for the child.

PART IV – COURT TACTICAL

CHAPTER 36:   FATHER IN COURT

There is a commonality of approach between preparing yourself for a custody fight in court and how to cultivate a long lasting sense of peace within yourself and a more harmonious relationship with your outer world. The type of father that a secular judge wants to hear about and observe on the witness stand is in many ways similar to the spiritual person all major mainstream religious and therapeutic traditions emulate. Both value certain traits of character, such as: the ability to foster and practice calm patience and understanding in the face of continuing hostility on the part of the mother of your child; and, having a good understanding and control on your own emotions. Search around in your day-to-day life and notice all the relationships you have on a regular basis. As good or as bad as they may be, pick one at a time and practice doing whatever it takes to improve it. It may sound corny, but just put a smile on your face and say "good morning" to someone you only pass by. Notice how you get a positive feeling about it. Spread the practice to other people. By doing this you will find it less difficult to deal with hostile people, including your ex.

At this moment, strongly resist the temptation to ignore this very simple practice by saying to yourself such simple ideas are of no real consequences to your ailments. There is no magical golden ring on the merry go-round. Practice mini steps, such as a charitable attitude toward your former spouse with no badmouthing of her or her family; turn the other cheek where appropriate; overcoming and getting beyond destructive emotional issues; and, have a desire to fix the problem and not the blame. How rare is it to see people concentrating on fixing the problem and not the blame. Learn to be one of those people. It takes humility and confidence, attributes important in court.

Cultivate a sincere understanding of the importance of

leaving the children out of the fight and not talking to them about legal issues. Keep the focus of your life on your children and don't bring them into the knowledge of another relationship you may have until that relationship is secure and you want it to be permanent. Understand the need to practice ethical and/or legal obligations, such as continuing to pay child support if legally bound to do so even in the face of the mother breaching court orders such as denying access.

These are just some of the values shared by most judges you will meet in family court. Your preparation for and participation in the court process should be seen as a dress rehearsal for the life long process which can follow: a dedicated practice of discovering and becoming the man you really want to be. Finding your soul. Many people not burdened by a marriage breakdown make it a goal at some point in their lives to do exactly that. Most don't get the chance to have a dress rehearsal as you do. Of course, no one would ever willingly volunteer to be in your shoes. But there you are, in your court shoes, never having thought that this unique juncture in your life was the perfect time to start seeking your path. You can kill two birds with one stone: help yourself and your kids to stay bonded, and start the exploration into the fields of self-discovery. To use a metaphor of the martial arts, you can take the unwanted forces being directed at you, place yourself in the right emotional position, bend those forces and use them to launch you forward in your own life.

Most men are like their children who, when asked post separation of their parents, how they would like things to be, answer "Let's all get back together!" That is an ideal whose time has passed. There is that longing, like an addict for another shot, to escape, if only temporarily, from the agony and fear of the moment back to the familiar dysfunctionality of the relationship. That way you could not only avoid the quick-sands of the legal process, but also wouldn't have to try and wrap your mind around the bizarre suggestion I am making that there is an unequalled opportunity now for self-discovery.

Guilt can be a powerful impediment to focusing clearly on the decision that must be made. It can stifle clear thinking on the question of whether or not to leave. After you leave it can haunt you for years if you don't do something about it. This is very common. Everyone, after abandoning any serious endeavor, thinks of many ways he might have been able to make it last, or how he could have and should have done better. This can be the case even where it was your partner, whom you may still have loved and wanted to live with, was the one who pulled the plug. But that is crying over barrels of spilt milk, and it gets you absolutely nowhere. No matter how confusing and how many loose ends your life is at, this is a pain you have to suffer. It is the price of admission into a new and far better future for you if you want it badly enough and are prepared to stick it out. This book is for men who are prepared to take that journey. You have to go down to the depths of grief, to the ashes of your lost life, and remain banished there until you glimpse the light of your soul disclosing a way back up.

It is true we all hear some really amazing stories of how two people who seemed totally antagonistic to each other somehow ended up reconciling and back together. It is like some terminal cancers go into remission without anyone ever knowing why. Some people actually win the lottery. The point I am driving at is this: if you and the mother of your child had what it takes to get back together the odds are you would be by now. Think about it: do you really want to go back from where you just escaped? And even if you did, would she be able to change, as you will have to, to make it work the next time? Do yourself a favor and turn those super-sized rear view mirrors on the shoulders of your mind sideways so they no longer block your forward vision. Get on with getting on with your new life. But as you do this, be very careful not to close and lock any doors that would forever prevent the extremely remote possibility that a miracle will happen and you might someday get back together with her. There is really a need to do anything that can irrevocably prevent reconciliation. If there is something you simply must do, can't avoid, for your children that risks guaranteeing no possible future reconciliation, then you must do it.

You are at a major crossroads and your options are few. Basically, there is the easier way out and the harder way out. The easier way is to the avoid the real issue. Side step. Deny. Bury yourself in pain numbing experiences like drinking, working too hard or a new woman, in short any dysfunctional approach except dealing with the reality head on. The harder way is to challenge and disrupt your old ways to create the space and opportunity for a healthy change. And only a changed person stands a chance of not repeating all the same mistakes that got you where you presently are.

So, take a few moments or a couple of days or as long as you need. Decide: is it going to be backward into a dysfunctional world of codependency and conflict, or forward into a new but uncertain future illuminated only by your commitment to self-discovery? It is safe to say, again, your reading of this book demonstrates your commitment forward.

There is a way out. This book is a guide to one way, the way that I have seen works well for fathers in separation. It certainly isn't the only way. There always have been multiple paths throughout civilization to achieve a goal. Finding your path is the goal. The goal is only roughly somewhere down the path. The magnificence of life is that we never really know where our path will lead.

> *"Most people spend more time and energy*
> *going around problems than trying to*
> *solve them." - Henry Ford*

CHAPTER 37: GETTING ORGANIZED FOR TRIAL

P reparing for the evidence you want to give and the questions you want to put to the mother and other witnesses is best organized by topic or history. Any allegation by you against the mother must by question be put to her also. Use different colored paper when preparing questions for the various witnesses on both sides, including yourself. As an example, suppose you want to testify that on a particular day the mother refused to let the child come out of her home to be picked up by you on your scheduled pick up time. Using blue sheets of paper for questions you will ask yourself, make a note of the question. Then write out the question for your ex alleging she refused to bring out the child on a pink sheet.

This way, at the end of a period of preparation you know that all the blue sheets must be organized in your binder for evidence you want to give, and the pink sheets should be organized by topic in a binder of cross-examination questions for the mother. Green, or some other color, are questions tone put to witnesses, yellow to psychologist or other experts.

When you are on the witness stand testifying make sure you go through all the blue sheets. When you are cross examining the mother make sure you go through all your pink sheets.

This method is especially useful in any circumstance where you have a multiple page document or custody report and you want to ask questions about and from it to more than one witness. You may have questions to put to the mother about the contents, and to the psychologist and to yourself or other witnesses.

If you have a 30-page custody report, reverse compile the pages. Take the first page and put it down text up and pile each subsequent page on top of the last. This will give you all the pages from highest numbered on top and page one on the bottom. Flip the pile over. Punch three holes in the right margin side of the bundle. Place in a three-ring binder. Place the pages on the right side of the rings. You should be looking down at the blank back side of the page one. Flip the page over so that it is facing up at you on the left side of the rings.

Then, with a yellow felt-tip marker start highlighting the sentences or portions of the report that you want to question someone on. Where you have more than one highlighted item on a page, take a red pen and number the sentence or paragraph. If the numbered sentence or paragraph raises questions you want to put to the mother, put a sheet of pink paper into the binder on the right side, place the number in the left side and write out the question you want to put to the mother. If the same sentence is something you want to address to the psychologist, put a yellow sheet in behind the pink, put the number in the left side and write out the question you want to ask of the psychologist. If you want to speak to the point yourself in your own evidence, put a blue sheet in with the point you want to make.

If there are other sentences or paragraphs on the same page, number them and go back to the pink and put the numbers to the left and write out your questions.

This way you have the original document pages on the left and your questions uncluttered written out on the right-hand pages.

The end result is a binder containing one or more multicolored sheets of questions. When the mother is on the witness stand you need only go to those pages on the left which have pink pages of questions on the right. It makes your questioning of witnesses and yourself much more orderly and easier not to forget.

If you have documents, such as an e-mail or letter or phone bill, that you want to refer to in connection with a question on your blue sheet or the mother's pink sheet, make note on the sheet referencing where in your material or court book of documents it can be found. Very important.

Before trial, organize all the documents you expect to rely upon in the trial in a tabbed book with an index. These documents could be photos, e-mails, school reports or anything else. You will have to make multiple copies for court purposes. One book of the original documents for the clerk to be used by a witness in the witness box, a copy for the judge, a copy for opposing counsel, and a copy for you.

The importance of getting physically organized for a hearing or a trial cannot be over emphasized. Nothing is more disconcerting or even embarrassing than to be addressing the court and unable to find this or that document. Or finishing up and having forgotten to make an important point because you didn't have the proper questioning in the right place in your organizing.

Trials are won in the preparation.

CHAPTER 38: AFFIDAVITS

There are two different ways to get an order from a judge. Everyone watches lawyers on TV argue before a judge or a jury in a trial. With some exceptions, the only way to get evidence before a jury is for a witness to take the witness stand, give an oath to tell the truth, and put in evidence through speaking or producing an identifiable document.

An actual trial usually occurs only when and if earlier preliminary court applications have failed to satisfy one or both parties.

The other way is in preliminary applications or hearings. The parties or their lawyers argue before a judge and the only evidence they refer to is what is sworn to in an affidavit. No witnesses take the stand. The lawyers can only refer to alleged facts if they are on the affidavits of their client and anyone supporting their client. The lawyers aren't supposed to allege anything that has not already been provided to the other side in an affidavit or is a response affidavit. This rule of practice restricts lawyers from what they can allege.

There are procedural rules which govern what should and should not be properly stated in an affidavit.

Wherever possible, you should speak from personal experience, i.e. what you saw or heard. If it is something you know, how do you know it? Where hearsay is allowed, detail who told it to you in what circumstances.

Remember the general evidentiary rule against hearsay. Hearsay is a statement made by someone who is not themselves swearing their own affidavit. Normally you cannot put forward or rely upon such a third-party statement. There are exceptions to the rule in family law. As in so many other areas of the rules of evidence, they pretty well fall apart in family cases.

You are always open to reporting what your children are

saying. How much weight the judge might put on any such statement depends upon the circumstances of your case.

Statements from third-party adults, if they are relevant, can be reported. Avoid double hearsay, such as telling what a third-party said they heard from a fourth party.

One significant benefit of representing yourself is that judges will let slide your breaches of evidentiary rules when they would hold a lawyer to a higher standard.

Be careful not to feign too much ignorance of the process when other aspects of your self-representation demonstrate that you do in fact know a great deal about the process. Your credibility will be shot.

An under-appreciated use of affidavits is that you can attach as exhibits to the affidavit any number of useful documents. These can be everything from copies of e-mails, letters, transcriptions of phone messages or taped calls, report cards, medical notes, birthday cards, employment records, family or other photographs, and anything else you want the judge to look at or hear.

Some psychologists divide people into two differing types when it comes to how we take in new information. Some of us are persuaded and learn more by concepts. Others are more influenced by image and photos. It is, therefore, always better to support a history of alleged facts with visual representations, be they documents or photos.

Whenever possible, be sure to attach photos of the children, you and the children, and ideally the mother and the children. Resist the tendency to include too many. A dozen total is sufficient. Pictures of you and the kids at sports, on vacation, and at Christmas are good. The best is often just hanging out. Depending on the age of the children, I suggest the dad get someone with a camera to take a couple of dozen quick shots of himself roughhousing with the kids on a couch or the floor. Typically at least one of the many shots will show a lovely, happy, smiling, bundle of   loving   activity.

CHAPTER 39: EVIDENCE

You may think you have all the facts in your favor. You sincerely believe that if anyone could see things the way you do, they would agree with you. And you are probably right. But it is all worthless if you can't produce evidence to not just tell your story but to prove it.

You are your own best story teller. When it comes your turn to take the witness stand, be prepared, and take as much time as you want. It is crucial not to give in to anyone's pressures that you finish soon, particularly the judge. Don't let fear of offending the judge cause you to not say what you want to say, and to call witnesses you want to call. The judge can be very intimidating. But it is your day in court. The judge is paid by the people.

All evidence should come from the voice of witnesses, either what the witness saw or heard or did, or by the production of documents that the witness can properly identify that connect to the issues of the case.

What you say on the witness stand is proper evidence. If it goes uncontested, it is proof not rebutted. If your statement is contradicted by the mother's evidence, the judge then has to decide which one of you to find the more credible and the less credible.

You are much better off if every important fact you want the judge to believe is backed up and supported by one or more other witnesses or documents. You alleged she threatened to keep the child from you. If you have it in an e-mail, on tape, or overheard by another person, introduce all that evidence. Nothing that supports you on even the slightest of issues should be neglected.

Expert witnesses, and reports from expert witnesses, can only be properly introduced into evidence by following special production rules in your jurisdiction. Be sure to learn them.

There will be moments when you ask yourself how much of what the mother has said, done or provided you should include in your own material or submissions. You have to use your intuition. On the one hand, you don't want to volunteer her accusations against you, or good things about herself. Let her provide that. Who knows, she may forget or overlook it. On the other hand, you don't want to be seen as trying to duck something obvious, and thereby have a judge think you might be trying to be a bit tricky.

Transcripts

Trial preparation is everything. It is trite to say, but oh so true. Ideally it should start the moment you see signs the marriage is over. But any time after that is okay too.

Reviewing any transcripts of earlier testimony, you may have given at a discovery or deposition is important for two reasons. Firstly, to be aware of your answers on the record to questions you are bound to be asked again at the trial. Equally as important as the content of the answers is the manner, style, and approach you took in framing your answers. It is always an education to read what we have said in such circumstances. We can see how infrequently we answer simple questions with a yes or no. The tendency to ramble shows itself.

Re-read any affidavits you have sworn to in the earlier proceedings. Remember your statements in the critical issues. Remember, if her lawyer points out a contradiction between your testimony and some early statement, be cool. Don't panic. While you take a moment to read your previous statement, if the lawyer absolutely has you, compose a calm apology and admission admitting an error. Underplay and hope it passes. However, if there is an actual honest explanation that can distinguish or explain the point, state it with equal understatement.

Read-ins

Some trial procedures permit one party to read to the judge as good evidence damaging statements from transcripts made by the other party in discovery or deposition. This can be a very effective tool. For you, it only works if you go first on the witness stand. If she goes first you can ask the same questions of her. If she changes her testimony from her early statements, you put the transcript to her and ask the great question: were you lying earlier or are you lying now?

If you go first in the trial, you have a great opportunity missed by most family lawyers. Let's assume that your ex's lawyer has been making a big deal in earlier court hearings that you are a bad dude. You now this is going to be a big theme in her testimony. She has sworn to police you hit it for no reason, without any provocation. She and her lawyer make that claim every chance they get. In her examination for discovery you got her to admit that she started the verbal argument. And she also admitted she made the first push. She started the fight.

You can expect her lawyer, when it is her turn to cross examine you, to try to make you agree with her client's side of the story, or get you confused so you can't be certain. But before that happens, you have the chance to pull the rug right out from under both of them. You can read in her transcript admission during your case, before the lawyer gets to cross examine you. You can do the same thing with as many comments in her transcript that will help your case and hurt hers. The result is that in addition to your evidence and the evidence of your witnesses, you have the mother's own evidence against herself. Her credibility is shot if, in her side of the trial, she testifies to her old story.

CHAPTER 40: HOW TO PROVE SOMETHING

Relevant evidence is used to prove a fact. Relevant evidence is "logically connected to the fact it is intended to establish"

You prove a fact by producing evidence which supports it. Evidence can be in the form of documents properly admitted as exhibits and oral testimony given under oath. The evidence can come in two forms: direct and circumstantial. Direct evidence is a properly sworn witness on the witness stand at trial, or in a sworn affidavit at a hearing. The witness should be able to say: "I saw the accused point the pistol at the deceased and shoot it and the deceased was hit and fell." Circumstantial evidence would be the same witness saying: "I saw the accused go into the room with a pistol in her hand. Then I heard a shot and when I came into the room I saw the deceased on the floor bleeding."

"Circumstantial evidence is evidence that relies on an inference to connect it to a conclusion of fact – like a fingerprint at the scene of a crime. By contrast, direct evidence supports the truth of an assertion directly – i.e., without need for any additional evidence or inference."

In family court, the rules of evidence frequently get bent, ignored, and abused. Judges admit statements and documents that shouldn't be allowed because the welfare of a child is involved. One of the significant benefits of representing yourself in court is that you are not expected to know those rules.

As in any other questions you might have at any time on any subject, always feel free to ask your judge how you should do something. To such requests judges sometimes respond by saying they can't give legal advice and you would be well advised to hire a lawyer. Don't let that phase you. Politely explain your predicament.

Fathers representing themselves worry about what they can and cannot say about their case to a judge. They shouldn't. Think only about telling your story as only you can. Let the mother's lawyer complain after the judge hears what you have to say. The worst that can happen is the judge will say that he or she will not put any weight on what they have heard. But they have heard it. If you have anything important to say, say it. The judge will understand it.

It is very important to repeat significant points of your evidence at least four times, preferably twice during your testimony and twice in your final argument at the end of the trial. Even if the judge suggests that he or she has your point, hammer it home again. There is nothing more maddening than to complete a hearing or trial and then to realize from the judge's reasons for judgment that they missed the point completely or got it backwards.

CHAPTER 41: ON BEING TRUTHFUL

Honesty is the best policy except when it isn't. All is fair in love and war. To win a military war can take deception, faking, and lying in creatively strategic ways. When up against a former spouse who resorts to deception, mistruths, untruths and extreme exaggeration the temptation to fight fire with fire is almost irresistible. If you succumb to that level as a knee jerk reflex you could seriously injure your case. Never attempt deception merely because the other parent dose. Even though fabricated evidence can be very effective in rare circumstances for specific purposes, I can't recommend you do it. That is a choice you will have to make for yourself, having measured all the possible consequences.

Parents with personality disorders need physical possession of their child to meet their own emotional needs. Their self-definition is founded on being the only person who can properly parent their child. They have totally convinced themselves the other parent is unfit and incapable. This line of thinking leads to a conviction the other parent is a danger to their child. Such a delusional parent rationalizes exaggerating and lying and false allegations against the other as required to protect the child. For that parent, it truly is warfare. Take no prisoners. Winning is everything, the child's necessary bond with the other parent be damned.

Where you are accused of several bad acts, all but one of which are false, admitting the true one but denying the false ones can be your best move.

May the gods help you if the other parent has an unethical lawyer riding shotgun.

CHAPTER 42: DIARIES

You must keep a diary or a journal. No matter how good your memory is, it will have lapses.

Diaries and journals kept in the traditional familiar way can be court-ordered produced as a relevant document. Where possible, it is important to get your hands on any diaries, journals, notes of computer records kept by the mother. There can be helpful information in them.

However, if you keep a diary for the very purpose of relying upon it at trial, it is categorized as litigation product and not producible. You don't have to show it to the other side. If it becomes known that you have a diary, say it was kept for the purpose of trial.

CHAPTER 43: TRIAL OPENING AND CLOSING

Think of the trial as a documentary movie about your life and current situation. Your opening is a trailer of what is to come. It tells the judge what you are seeking and what your witnesses and evidence are going to testify to, what you are going to prove.

If you open first, as you review your case take advantage of telling the judge what the other side is alleging and what evidence you will call to refute it.

The closing is a view back to all the things that went your way and against the mother's. Your closing is your argument where you finally get the chance to put it all together to tell the judge what is best for the child, and which parent has proven to the court on a balance of probabilities to be more in tune with the child and its world and future.

Delivering Your Opening Statement

Delivering an opening statement at the beginning of the trial is the first important step you have to take. If you are the claimant and go first, you have the right to make an opening. If you are the respondent and present your case after the mother's case, you may or may not have the right to make an opening statement at the very beginning of the trial. Otherwise you will have to wait until it is your turn to call evidence, after the mother's case and her witnesses are completed.

If you go second, it is still very important to try and get the court to permit you to make an opening before the mother begins her case. Don't be embarrassed to ask the judge for the opportunity to let him/her know what they should be looking for in the mother's case so that they will better understand your evidence when the trial turns to your part of the case.

Openings are supposed to be only a statement of the facts you expect to call and the orders you seek. Openings are not to be argument. However, it is hard not to put some argument in and it is actually helpful to the extent that you can get away with it. An advantage to representing yourself is that you can put some argument in your opening and the judge is less likely to call you on it than if your lawyer was saying it.

Remember, an opening is not evidence. Anything important you say in your opening you will have to independently introduce into evidence in the trial or it will have no importance.

If you are the respondent, there is an additional importance to having the judge hear your opening before the mother starts to give her evidence. If the mother goes first, the best way to thwart and defend against expected false testimony is to get your own version and facts out before the mother actually takes the stand to testify. This you can do with your opening.

There is an old adage that first impressions are the strongest. As in most such sayings, there is an opposite adage: He who talks last has an advantage. Who really knows? However, if you are the respondent, and will have your witnesses on the stand after the mother's. You can get a shot at giving the judge the first impressions you want him/her to have by reading your opening. It is not just a chance to put forward the theory of your case, but to undermine the mother's before she even gets to testify. You can pull the rug out from under her, so to speak.

The role of the mother's lawyer is to get her to give evidence that paints her as good, right and believable. The lawyer will have the mother and other witnesses paint you the opposite before you will have any chance to let the judge know otherwise from your own evidence. If you can give your opening after your ex's lawyer and before they start their case, you get to let the judge know the negative facts you intend to call against the mother.

Speak from your heart as the parent of the child. Just tell your story. Tell the child's story.

If you have smoking gun evidence against her, put it squarely into your opening.

After the lawyer for the mother has completed reading their opening to the judge, and before they call their first witness – and you interrupt them if they are quicker than you – and ask the judge in just these words:

"Judge – would it help to hear my opening at this point? I request I may deliver it now."

There may be an earlier opportunity to raise it with the judge. Grab it.

When it is your turn to take the witness stand and give your testimony it will only be natural for you to mix opinions and argument in with your recitation of facts. That is very normal for self-representing parents. From time to time the judge may remind you to try and stick to facts and leave argument for the end of the trial. It is good to try and follow that advice as best you can. You won't hurt your case by braking the rule from time to time.

You have a better opportunity to make argument during the trial when you are cross examining the other parent or their witnesses. You can challenge their opinions and views. You can state your own opinions and views and arguments provided you always ask if they agree. There has to be a question   somewhere.

CHAPTER 44: CROSS EXAMINATION

Methods of asking questions of a witness in a trial are of two types: cross examination or leading questions, and direct examination.

When a party is questioning their own witnesses, they are not allowed to cross examine. They cannot lead their witness to the answer they seek. That party can only cross examine the other party's witnesses.

A party must only conduct direct examination of their own witnesses. Unless you can come at it from another direction, you are more or less stuck with the answer you get.

Direct examination questions are open ended. Why, when, where and how type of questions. You may or may not know the answer. What did you do last Christmas? The answer you seek must not be contained in the question. Answer: We went to Disneyland. Under cross examination, the same question would be worded like this:

Cross examination question: You went to Disneyland last Christmas, did you not?

Answer: Yes.

The answer is contained in the question. If you don't get the answer you like, you can cross examine the witness vigorously to try and get them to give you the answer you need. Good cross examination is a skill. You may have that skill. Do some research on cross examination styles.

Courtroom lawyers must be very careful in how they question a witness or they will get challenged by opposing counsel or the judge. Many lawyers don't fully understand the rule and often get called on it. Acting as your own lawyer, you benefit from judges not expecting lay litigants to understand the rule on cross examination. Ask any way you want until the judge decides you need a lesson on how to do it. Don't worry about such a mild reprimand. It will not take away from your case. Just don't abuse it. A judge may give less weight to answers from leading questions asked during direct examination.

Don't be shy about objecting to opposing counsel when you think they are cross examining their own witness. Stand up from your seat. The judge should then recognize you wish to say something. Just say you object to the manner of questioning. It is not unusual when a witness is first called to the stand for the lawyer to ask them leading questions about who they are, age, job, etc., and to confirm some basic background. That is cross examination. But when the questions turn to the issue of the trial, they must stop.

Of course when you take the witness stand and give you own evidence, feel totally free to say it any way you wish. Just tell your story.

Most importantly, don't feel rushed. Don't let anyone or thing make you feel rushed. Take as much time as you need. This is your day in court.

CHAPTER 45: THE OPPOSING LAWYER

Try not to personalize hostility in the person of the mother's lawyer. It is very easy to think the lawyer is as much or more of the problem as the mother. Focusing too much on the antics, allegations, and false statements of the lawyer takes your eye off the ball. If the mother's lawyer steps so far beyond what is acceptable, and other lawyers agree with you, then you should write a formal complaint to that lawyer's governing body. Don't expect much. We lawyers protect our own. But at least your letter will be in that lawyer's file, and maybe more will follow or have preceded you.

Governing bodies send your complaint to the lawyer and ask for a response. You should get a copy of that response. Often there are admissions that are interesting. The lawyer might even be compelled to cease representing the mother.

In the meantime, focus on the tasks at hand. Unless the lawyer's behavior is way over the top, the lawyer is not the task at hand.

CHAPTER 46: DELAY

Delay is always something to be sought or avoided. It should not be regarded as a neutral factor in your planning.

With some exceptions, it is hardly ever that you want to actively work to delay a hearing or trial. That is typically what the mother and her lawyer try to do. The longer they can preserve her status quo advantage with the children, the more difficult they think it will be for you to change. Often, the mother is in the matrimonial home and has no incentive to leave. It is usually to her financial advantage to remain.

Some causes for delay are outside the control of either party. A common one in some jurisdictions is when there are more trials to commence on the expected date than there are judges available. The civil servants in the courthouses who schedule trials book more than one for each Monday. History provides a ratio of trials booked to trials that settle out of court. Statistically there are times when there are little or no settlements. A shortfall of available judges or courtrooms result.

You can help yourself by contacting the office in charge of assigning judges to upcoming trials. Find out how long before your trial date they will be assigning a judge. If it sounds as though you may be in competition with other commencing trials, take the opportunity to lay out why your trial should be given priority. Key in that list is the significant need to resolve the issues around your child. Maybe there is a deadline to decide what school the child is going to attend, where the parents are going to live, financial demands that require resolution, etc. Tell them if there has already been an adjournment of an earlier trial date.

Don't be bashful in expressing your need. Remember, the person you are talking to feels under paid and over work. Respect the civil servant. Get their sympathy. The problems, inequities, and unfairness of the system are not their fault.

It is a good investment of your time to befriend the clerks at the court registry desk handling your file. They can be a real help as you try and navigate the labyrinth of the court process of forms, setting dates and filing documents. They have learned to be frontline help to many fathers just like yourself who are acting without lawyers.

It is impossible not to be bitterly disappointed if a trial date desperately sought gets delayed. It is human nature. A delay may have been sought by the other side. Or a delay may be perceived by you as an unfair advantage to the other side. As you organize your file and prepare for trial, always bare in the mind the possibility of delay. Personally, I trained myself early on in my career to view every unwanted delay as an opportunity. It is an opportunity, in so many ways, to get better prepared. Take a few minutes, an hour, or even a day to vent your anger and frustration. Then buckle down hard on getting back to work on your case.

CHAPTER 47: COURT-ORDERED
ASSESSMENTS AND EXPERTS

All jurisdictions have rules of practice providing for a mental health professional to prepare an evaluation of the family dynamics for the court. They can be prepared by civil servant social or justice workers, normally for free. More thorough and knowledgeable ones are done by psychologists or the rare psychiatrists who are qualified to administer and interpret personality inventories. These higher qualified are a must when dealing with a personality disordered mother. The resulting written assessment is to guide the judge on the best interest of the child.

Extreme caution must be exercised in determining which expert to agree to or put forward to the court. All the risks of gender bias discussed in this book apply in spades to mother-centric psychologists, of which there are still too many. The other side will suggest names they think will favor their side. Do your own research. Find the names of some divorce lawyers who are known for doing well for dads. Ask them for the names of their preferred expert. Go to a law library and ask staff help you find recent family cases where various experts have testified. Find out what they said and how their evidence was taken. Go to the internet.

Find a courthouse with a family case where such an expert will testify. Sit in. It will be a valuable education.

Your Experts

Court-ordered custody evaluations by specialists can be very expensive. A much less expensive way is to hire your own expert. You simply provide that person with all the facts of your case but call them hypotheticals. Don't give real names. Just be certain that every hypothetical you can prove with evidence at trial. After listing all the hypotheticals, you then pose the key questions: on the basis of the hypotheticals, would equal time shared parenting be appropriate for this child? And other such questions.

Expect the mother, through her lawyer, to defend against such an expert report by claiming the expert never heard the mother's side. To protect against that, before having your expert start the report, tell the mother what you intend to do and invite her to participate. She won't. Then you point that out.

Check with any local fathers or shared parenting groups for their advice on names of fair experts who support shared parenting in the appropriate circumstances.

CHAPTER 48: SPLIT ISUES

Most family court litigation involves more than one substantive issue. In some cases, there comes a time when one side or the other suggests that there be a preliminary determination by a judge on a single subject before having a trial or hearing on other subjects. Unless it is really a no-brainer without serious consequences if you lose, such applications are generally to be resisted. The temptation to resolve something, to remove an irritant, to simplify things and to reduce the time and effort required for what is left, can be overwhelming, particularly if a smooth-talking lawyer for the mother is trying to sell you on it.

If it is important you not lose sight of the point at issue: your odds and chances of convincing a judge of your position are greater in a full hearing or trial of all the issues. Only in that fashion can the judge get the full spectrum picture of all the facts, including most importantly who you are. Short, segregated one-issue hearings don't allow for you to fully educate the judge as you are in a full hearing or trial.

CHAPTER 49: DISCOVERY AND DEPOSITION

Cardinal rule # 1: Say as little as possible. Ideally nothing. But that is not possible. "Yes" and "no" can usually suffice.

Rule # 2: Tone down your language, adjectives, and descriptive terms of your ex. By all means, if asked, describe her behavior. Let the trial judge form his/her own words to describe her behavior.

Rule # 3 – Don't be judgmental! Don't be accusatory. Hate the sin but love the sinner.

Rule # 4 – Never ever express an opinion or make an argument unless very specifically requested to.

Rule # 5 – Only answer the question asked. Resist the temptation to answer what you think the follow up question will be. That question may never come.

It is helpful to understand the litigation process as a play, a piece of complex theater. All the participants have their role to play, a script to learn and follow, and your place on the stage.

It is only natural that you might now view a discovery examination as your chance to finally tell your side of the story. Your opportunity to set the record straight.

No, no, no, no.

Such an approach could be a disaster!

I am the director of your play. I am giving you your script. In discovery or deposition your role is to be an actor very different from who you really are and would like to come across as. This is not a normal life event. This is the opposing counsel's big chance to attack. To come out with as little blood on you as possible, you have to stick to the script.

I was examined once. I experienced the incredible natural urge to abandon the script my lawyer gave me and to break out and just be my argumentative self. I had the sense that I must be seen by the people in the room as a stick figure, not free to be the person I wanted to see myself as. Who I was, what I was, the real me, was being denied. And that is exactly what it should have been.

At the end of the discovery, all that remains is a written transcript. There is no audio or video record. No one will ever hear or see how you answered your questions.

I thought I had been the perfect client. Reading the transcript I was astounded at how often I talked too much.

Only if this matter ends up in a trial will you finally have an opportunity to tell your side of the story. Hopefully, your case will not need to go to trial. It can be settled. One of the things that you have to give up if you want to settle without trial is your opportunity to get your story out. Your priority is not to get your side of the story out. Your priority is to try and settle the case to the best result for your children.

Please read and re-read this section so that it sinks deeply into your understanding.

Perhaps the best reasons to conduct a discovery against your ex is to get a practice run at her. For a man unaccustomed to have to dig for information from an opposing party, it can be frustrating and unproductive. You often never get from her what you regard as the truth. That is one of the most infuriating of moments, when you see the judge accepting the very false, totally subjective image she has created. And now it is your turn. You are up at bat. And unlike her, you have objective facts to support your analysis of what is going on. Where she relied on emotion and a lot less than the whole truth, you will use objective evidence to build and win your case. That is what your whole post separation life has been focused on to this moment. Feeling only slightly nervous or really fearful, you rise to your feet. You are about to jump into a pond over your head.

The kind judge is helping to give you some floatation by explaining the trial process. It is helpful. You start. For a fraction of a moment, you are back in the dream where you are screaming out but no sound can be heard.

What I have just described is toward the fear end of the spectrum. Certain fathers from commerce, industry, business, etc. come into their own trial itching for the fight. It is rare to see such a man representing himself. They can afford lawyers and experts.

The discovery process offers you the chance to practice cross examining your ex in a situation where not a great deal is at risk. Mistakes usually stay in the room. It can become button pushing combat. You have each become masters of button pushing. Women almost always win such a contest. Be ready for the more subtle and devious aspects of her behavior to come when being pressed for an answer by you. You may also strike an honest chord. When that happens, if what she is testifying to is helpful to you expand upon it.

Have a good female friend pretend to be her lawyer cross examining you.

Do a lot of that until you have good answers for the difficult questions.

After several hours of cross examination, you will be much more prepared for the time in the trial when you will be cross examined. Then switch roles with her becoming your ex and you cross examine her.

Practice   makes   perfect.

CHAPTER 50: DISCLOSURE

There are rules that require both sides in a family court case to let the other side know what documents you have in your possession that relate or could relate to the issues in the case. This applies to all documents, not just the ones that you intend to rely upon. The general principal is that you are not supposed to hide some document and ambush the other with it in court.

Rules of court and practice aim at insuring that both sides in a court case have access to the documents and information of the other side before actually going into a hearing or trial. This is particularly so in the superior courts. The lower family courts often are not as strict. The authors of the court rules decided that full and complete and early disclosure of all documents might help settle cases, once both sides see the ammunition the other side has.

One aim of document disclosure is to force each side to see the good and bad aspects of their and the other side's case. What courts don't like is for one side to hide some smoking gun piece of evidence and then bring it out in court to ambush the other side. Such practice is regarded as unfair. But of course fairness is a term not always applied to how the courts treat children and fathers. Mothers and their lawyers who find themselves in a high contest custody case are less concerned with fairness than winning. The truth is not something they always seek to disclose but is often something they seek to hide. A father up against a personality disordered or victim-feminist wife will too often get shellacked by being fair in the court process.

Financial Disclosure
It is a requirement in family law proceedings that each side prepare and file and exchange financial disclosure documents. Such disclosure is often a sworn document. Obviously, great care and attention should go into the

preparation of any such documents. They should be prepared in the full expectation that you will be cross examined on the document at some later stage in the litigation. Mothers' lawyers, with little else of substance to go after you on, frequently try to make mountains out of molehills in pointing out discrepancies in your financial documents. They will try to paint you as a dishonest person for merely having over estimated an expense here or a bank balance there. If this should happen, don't hit the panic button. Simply admit to an oversight or misunderstanding of what you were being requested to provide. Look the lawyer in the eye and calmly await his or her next question.

Depositions and Examination for Discovery

Court rules in most superior courts provide that each party (or their lawyer) can take the other party into a room with a court reporter, put the opposing party under oath, and then cross examine them on the issues in the case. If you get good admissions that help your case or hurts hers, a transcript can then be prepared by the court reporter. That transcript has a couple of important functions. You can use it as evidence in pre-trial hearings. At trial you can use it to cross examine her if her evidence differs from the transcript.

Good lawyers will demand that they have all the relevant documents on the case before agreeing to submit their client to be cross examined by the other side. If a document is produced and put to their client that they have not seen before, they may object to it being examined on until they have had time to consider it. Many lawyers make no such objection. It is raised here as an example of an advantage to not disclosing a document before the questioning. Example: You have an audio recording of the mother telling you that if you don't make the month's child support payment you don't get the kids for the weekend. You delay disclosing that recording. In the discovery or deposition questioning, you ask her if she has ever said any such thing. She denies it. Thereafter you can produce the tape and use it in a later hearing or at trial to impeach her credibility. Remember though, the existence of that tape must be disclosed to the other side before you will be able to produce it in court. It has to be listed on your list of documents. Don't wait until just before court to disclose its existence.

It is very important that you press hard to get as much information as possible the other side has. This includes tax returns, bank and credit card monthly statements, medical records etc. Diaries and journals. Medical and phone records. Every court has a set of rules which detail how you can force the production of such documents.

Gamesmanship

Delay in disclosing certain of your smoking gun documents or information is a well know tactic among lawyers. The question which I can only help you decide, but which you will ultimately have to decide for yourself, is what ammunition to disclose soon and which to hold in reserve. It is true that early disclosure of certain types of evidence can move the mother and her lawyer in the direction you want. If they don't move as far as you want, if you have shot your load, you have no arrows left in your quiver. If you know that no matter how much ammo you discharge in her direction she will still remain stubborn, that is when it is important to have some good stuff in reserve. The other side will not know what you have. That is the time to try and get them on the record as denying something you can prove.

Remember that sooner or later before trial, you must disclose. If you don't disclose and end up in court and spring it on them, you run a great risk it might get excluded as evidence. It is important that sooner rather than later you check with the rules of evidence and court practices in your jurisdiction to find out how judges deal with ambush evidence in family court.

CHAPTER 51: COMMUNICATION BREAKDOWN

"The void created by the failure to communicate is soon filled with poison, drivel and misrepresentation." - C. Northcote Parkinson

Holding meaningful conversations with your wife before separation was likely difficult and is most likely going to be more so after separation. Some post-separation relationships are so toxic there can be no communication at all. Obviously, it's important not to let this happen.

Our education system takes few steps to teach students how to conduct conversations. Ex partners in a childless relationship could theoretically spend the rest of their lives never needing to communicate. However, children deserve to have parents who, if not now, eventually can treat and communicate with one another with respect.

If you and your former partner have an inability to communicate effectively, make it a high priority to get her to join you in getting help from a communications coach or counselor.

CHAPTER 52:   LETTERS AND E-MAILS

Every communication you make is capable of being brought up in court either as a shot at your ex or to your benefit. This includes reports, letters, notes, diaries, etc. It includes e-mail and text messaging. It includes messages left on answering machines. It includes recordings made between you and another, either with or without your knowledge.

Every communication you send to anyone should be viewed from two perspectives: be brief, polite, and to the point , and how will it look if produced by either side in court? Every communication received by you from any source should be viewed as a possible document to be used by you in court. Either to advance your case, or diminish the mother's. Where credibility is a significant issue between the parents, communication documents can be a useful weapon in your quiver. It is never too early to start regarding your communications with the keen eye of a father out to help his children.

Your e-mails to her should be controlled, adult, polite, non-judgmental. Don't argue or beg. Her's to you are a possible window into the manifestation of whatever remains hidden within and to her.

Every letter you write must serve two distinct purposes. The first is an attempt to explain, obtain, or respond to a specific matter; to cause something to happen or not happen. Second, as important as the communication might be for its immediate purpose, it could take on greater significance should your case actually go to trial. It can be used by you in the cross examination of the mother. It can also be used against you by the opposing lawyer.

Everything you do as part of your case must be viewed as how it might look if you end up before a judge. Every corner of your life and detail of your litigation is open for cross-examination by the mother's lawyer. As is hers by you.

Therefore, all communications by you to anyone involved should, if accepted as evidence and read by the trial judge, put you in the best light possible. Most people never think of this early on when they say and write things with no expectation it will be seen again. Tape recordings of phone conversations or messages left can also be used to great effect in cross-examination.

Any early statement by the mother that exhibits anger, irrationality, arrogance, stubbornness, a sense of entitlement, inflexibility or putting herself above the interests of your children, can be used against her. And any document that shows you being conciliatory, rational, putting the children ahead of yourself, and not holding grudges will obviously help you.

Some mothers can be goaded into putting extreme comments in communications. Mother's with personality disorders, such as borderline, in public and court can come across as totally rational, sensible, and believable. It is in private communications that you catch them displaying their pathology.

It is important you understand the importance of these self-serving communications from you to her. It is important you take this advantage in writing to the mother or her lawyer very early on and then from time to time. If your case doesn't settle, and you end up in the gauntlet of a courtroom, those older communications can be brought out and put to the mother. You can challenge her on her positions. You can ask her what she thought of your positions? Make her try to justify her objections to your ideas, which by the time of trial may be accepted by the judge as good ones. And hers as bad ones.

Such letters can't just be you saying what a great guy are. If you put your version of an event that is in dispute, in a communication, your version is not evidence. That sort of self-serving statement is not allowed. Your testimony from the witness stand is your evidence of the event.

All is not fair in the love and war over children.

A Controlled Response

Remember that e-mails can be produced in trial as documentary evidence by the person to whom it was sent. You want to make sure that your e-mails contain nothing that can be used against you. If you know what gets under her skin and gets her disordered personality to surface, go for it. Even better, get it on tape if you can.

You must resist the urge to let off steam in response to a hostile e-mail. First, determine if the e-mail requires any response at all. If it does, be brief. Very brief. Every time you take the bait and argue back all you are doing is feeding her anger habit.

There are exceptions. For example, if you and the mother attend at school and meet with your child's counselor, and she then sends you an e-mail with a false version of what occurred and was said, you should respond with a matter of fact statement of your memory of the meeting and leave it at that. If she comes back with an argument, ignore it. You are already on the record. That's enough.

Remember to watch what you say on social media, and search for what she is saying.

Never assume you have any privacy.

Stay Calm and Carry On

The rubber hits the road when there are incoming e-mails oozing sarcastic, passive-aggressive put-downs. There might even be a gem that really proves an important point at issue. Regardless of what comes in, what goes out by you must be super cool. Your watchdog of emotional correctness should supervise any venting of your most negative pain. Everyone is entitled to some uncharacteristic acting out at the moment of realizing the floor was about to fall out from under you. Recapturing that escaped emotional acting out is absolutely critical. Just apologizing doesn't cut it. Reform. You have to be all those things your grandmother told you she was absolutely certain would turn you out a bright and handsome young man with all the attributes to be a gentleman. That was her hero ideal for her grandson. How much did she get right?

Subduing your emotions about your ex is an antidote for much of what ails you. Take a blood oath with yourself not to breach the walls of steely self-control you feel is within you. In this worst of fate's circumstances, you must locate and resuscitate the will power to be true to who you want to become.

Did you ever think you wanted to be a priest or Tibetan monk committed to compassion? Well this is your chance to practice with your ex. Be warned and don't let it stop you: Your very first attempt will be a revelation on how hard it is going to be to put into practice what you wished of the world. Recovering your soul is life's toughest journey.

Many high-conflict parents of both genders engage in e-mail war. Dozens in one day. All hours of the night and day. You make a big mistake when you send back what you think is a very commonsense counter argument bomb to her indefensible position. All you are doing is fueling her appetite to struggle for control. Just stop it. You will see when you don't respond to her argumentative emotions and put downs it often leaves very little or nothing that requires your attention and response.

If your personal experience suddenly seems not so bad after reading some of this book, I am glad for you. You have a big leg up to maybe benefit from a semi-peaceful resolution of your separation. Your children will do better in life. But if this is your story, be a centurion for your children.

CHAPTER 53: SPOUSAL SUPPORT

Aclaim against you for spousal support can be both the most difficult to defend against, and often the most unfair of all results short of losing your children.

She pleads poverty. She has tried so hard to find work. She wants more schooling. As part of the pitch for more schooling she will usually tell the judge that if only she could have two more years of school – paid for by you – she is confident she could just walk out into the workforce and find a well-paying job.

Then it is your turn to cross examine her. Here is where you have to make a serious ninja move. You may regard your ex as less than fully motivated to get out and help support herself and your child. You fully believe she is basically selfish and lazy. You may be right. But for the moment, in that courtroom, on that stage, you want to sing the praises of her energy, ingenuity, and will power. Tell what an energetic entrepreneur she can be if she wants to. Build her capacity for work up as high you can.

The trick is to get her to commit to being able to make an income fairly soon and not after three years of "basket weaving" college. Show her how it can be done. Do your research.

If she used to have employment before children came, say teaching, early on in the separation start researching the employment opportunities in that field. Gather up employment sections of the newspapers, job placement web sites, and bulletins from the union of teachers. From time to time send them to her lawyer. Don't overdo it.

Those same notices can be attached to an affidavit and placed before a judge in any hearing she might bring for spousal support. At examination for discovery or deposition you can put them in front of her and ask if she inquired into any them. Become an expert on the subject of employment in her field, or any other she has the skills for. At trial you effectively point out to the judge that she isn't serious   about   working.

CHAPTER 54: GAME THEORY

If all else along the way fails, you are left with only the trial. Everything you do along the way, from the moment you think there is going to be court action, until the very day of the trial, should have one objective: have as much ammunition as you possibly can assemble for the trial when and if it comes. And you can only get what you want if you have evidence to support yourself. From day one you must begin collecting and organizing the evidence. Find it if you don't have it. Every e-mail, ever phone call, every comment in court, must be viewed ultimately be from the perspective of the trial judge.

An analogy: you want to build a house at a time and location not yet determined. You prepare. You assemble all the materials you will need, and the tools to build with. When the day does come to actually build your house, all the bricks you have assembled will do you no good at all if you forgot the water for the cement to hold the bricks together.

Think backwards from the future date of a trial back to the present. Reverse engineering. Determine what it will take at the trial. Make a list of all the component parts of a successful trial. Then create a schedule setting out a process and time frame for securing all the essential documents and witnesses you will need to prove your case.

There is a name for the process of establishing your goal, and then working to put all the pieces in place to achieve it: game theory. Research it. It is a valuable theory/tool   to   help   in   your   fight.

CHAPTER 55: OUTSIDE COURTROOM AGREEMENTS

You have heard the expression that some legal fights only get settled on the court house step. It is true. The interview room across the hall from the courtroom is an unappreciated location for forging agreements. Nothing so focuses one's eye on the moment than knowing that across the hall a total stranger in a robe sits up on his chair dictating how the lives of previous lovers will unfold. The interview room is the last stage before that foreign arena. The last chance.

Few litigants head off from their lawyer's office prepped for a possible critical meeting in the interview room. Few lawyers who do manage to get their client and the mother and her lawyer seated at the table in the interview room come equipped to appreciate and take advantage of the psychological pressure on the mother at that moment and that location. Many good opportunities get missed. Each side has placed many if not all their chips, financial and emotional, on this legal roll of the dice. Bluffs and gambles at the ready. She stakes everything on her champion lawyer being better armed than the father in the weapons of argument. No matter the confidence her lawyer has sold her, she may have doubt. And doubt is what you need to cultivate in her.

Doubt suggests to her ego that she may suffer a loss. Her ego can't tolerate that thought. Compromise may still seem a dirty word for her when it comes to her enmity toward the father, but being a loser hurts worse. Causing her doubt is your best weapon.

How to Utilize Doubt

If you are trying to talk a fundamentalist of any religion out of some of their more radical superstitions by using rationality, good luck! But if you can simply raise some doubt on one or more of their underlying assumptions, you have opened the door a crack. Work on opening it more.

Failure to agree, failure to compromise, failure even to negotiate, demand to fix the blame and not the problem, drive the systems agenda to get you into court. Last offers at settlement have failed. That is no reason not to enter the courthouse unprepared for the possibility of further negotiations.

It pays to scout out the courthouse in advance. Find where there may be an interview room. On the day of your hearing, take advantage of any waiting, break or delay to suggest a sit down in the interview room. Be proactive in that. If at any time during any hearing, if the judge asks if the parties might want to take a break and consider their position, always agree. You just never know.

If you do manage to reach an agreement with your ex, have it written by her lawyer. Inspect every word, every sentence. Make sure each sentence clearly states the agreed terms and can't be interpreted later in some other fashion. Don't sign it until have it reviewed by a lawyer of your choice. Once an agreement has been reached, ask a judge to turn the agreement into an order. Between the signing of the agreement and a judge making it an order your ex can change her mind. As can you.

CHAPTER 56: NO TURNING BACK

So, you're getting divorced and need to learn how to navigate the ins and outs of the court system. One of the first things you'll find out is that the courts love paperwork. Dot your "i's and cross your "t's, get affidavits, fill out forms, make applications, file notices, file responses, make motions, go to court hearings just to set a date for a court hearing. The list is seemingly endless and if you forget to sign your name at the bottom, you can start all over again.

Securing equal parenting time is an uphill battle for fathers. Realistic fathers go into the legal arena knowing the cards are stacked against them. Setbacks are to be expected along the often lengthy legal path. Many interim applications may have to be made, often extending over months if not years.

There is no more disheartening and defeating moment than losing an important custody or parenting schedule application early on or mid-way through the litigation. This often happens for a number of possible reasons. Keep your spirits up and learn from each setback. Interim orders are not final. The more ground you lose in the beginning the more likely you will have to go to trial. You might even come out of an interim application worse off than going in. When the idea of just quitting raises its ugly head, don't give up. Remember you are doing this for your children.

The simple fact is that there are just some cases that can never be properly dealt with in anything other than a full trial with witnesses and experts called to testify and where you can test evidence through cross-examination. Only in the fulcrum of this age-old process may the rights of your children get the full hearing they deserve.

After a serious setback on an interim application there are basically 3 options:

- Appeal. This is more time and money and the odds of success usually slight.
- Make a new application. With the passage of time, you can rearrange your tackle and, depending upon the rules in your jurisdiction, bring on a fresh application based on new circumstances.
- Go to trial. The pain of missing your children will be unbearable but this is often the best use of limited funds.

What you should not do is not give up.

It's possible that, having won one or more early applications, your ex and her lawyer might feel overly confident and let their guard down. They might roll into the trial process expecting to win again. They may put less effort into the trial than you can. You can lose battles and still win the war.

If, on the other hand, you've been the successful party going into trial remember to not start celebrating until you've crossed the finish line.

Keep focused on what the judges care about. They don't care if you feel your ex is embittered, miserable, lying, manipulative and lazy. They care about the best interests of the child. Spend your time focused on proving you serve the best interests of your child and less time trying to show how your ex is a nasty, vindictive swindler. Document when she does things that harm their interests. Keep your personality conflicts out of the courtroom.

CHAPTER 57: COSTS

Certain court jurisdictions provide for an award of dollar costs after a trial against an unsuccessful parent in favor of the more successful parent.

An emblematic example of the continuing gender bias in the family court system is the disproportionate ratio of costs awarded against fathers as against mothers in equal outcomes.

It is important for judges to fairly meet out costs against those mothers who abuse society's desire to see children shared equally between separated parents wherever possible.

Costs now are a disincentive to fathers to stand up in court for the rights of their children.

Be sure to check in your jurisdiction what the rules are with respect to costs. If cost can be awarded in your case, go to the local law library. Ask for help in finding cases or a text on the subject. Study it. It is not that complicated.

During any final negotiations before your court date, don't forget to factor in costs if you are not successful.

CHAPTER 58:   IN CLOSING

"No one can cheat you out of ultimate
success . . . but yourself." - Ralph Waldo
Emerson

For years I have been discovering and reading books and articles on parenting, child psychology and pedagogy. Gone to numerous conferences on the subject. Over the past few decades a whole new industry has developed on the subject of how to raise kids. Everyone and their aunt has something to say and wants to be heard. Among all the pop psychology there has been some very good work done by experts.

No one has more simply and elegantly put forward a theory than the English pediatrician and psychoanalyst Donald Winnicott. He was at his height in the 1950's. Today no one has heard of him. There can be no better foundation for parenthood than his plain message. There can be no better theme for a parent in trial to espouse on behalf of their children. There can be no better litigation strategy than to demonstrate with evidence how the other parent violates Winnicott's principles and thus the child.

Here, from a lost source, is a very brief overview of his theory:

When parents are too inclusive or too abandoning in the way that they relate to their children, when the parents are too invested or not invested enough that creates a circumstance for the child where they can no longer just be. They instead have to rise to the location and create a caretaker self. To create a caretaker self to manage either the intrusive or the abandoning demands of the parent. This caretaker self is tinged with a self of falseness -a false self-that obscures that capacity to feel real. There is an additional optimal stance-good enough parenting-not too intrusive and too abandoning.

The parent doesn't have to be perfect-just has to be good enough, and that good enough attention permits the child to be able to be alone in the presence of another. The child can be playing by himself with the parent present but in the background. This provides good enough ego coverage. The child can float free in his or her emotional experience or in their own play. They have the capacity to process emotions or just play to feel free.

But when this doesn't happen, what comes instead is premature thinking that is embodied in the caretaker's self. The child is rising up out of the emotional body into their mind trying to figure out how to manage the demands of the depressed parent, or the angry parent, or the aloof parent, or the withdrawn parent, or the needy parent.

The left over damage of that kind of drama is a residue sense of unworthiness, of never having been seen as who one was what might have been, whatever that might have been.

They feel discomfort with dwelling in that place where a child with good enough parents can dwell naturally.

Agony emerges from childhood when there is too much emphasis in taking care of one's parent and this inability to bear one's own feelings, to bear the intensity of one's own feelings because those feelings are precisely those of the parent who is unable to let the child have their own. What comes out of that kind of childhood experience is a sense of estrangement or disassociation.

I find this theory applicable to almost every case I have ever had.

If this theory clicks with you, go on line and learn more of this pioneer's ideas.

Look back at your own childhood. Were your parents good enough? Did they let you just be? Or did you have to care for the emotions of one or both of them? Could that have played a role in your own creation of a false hero? Was that the beginning of ignoring your own young soul?

The court room is a theater stage upon which the actors speak their parts. Your job is to gather the facts and write your own script. Memorize your lines. Set the stage and step out from the wings confident that the love for your children and theirs for you will earn an ovation. If you jumble your lines, let your heart do the talking.

As they say in the theater business: "Break a leg!"

ABOUT THE AUTHOR

Carey Linde is a Vancouver-based family lawyer who has been practicing law since 1972. He is a single father of three and grandfather of 4.

Carey pioneered the movement for equal-time shared parenting in the courts of Canada. His practice is aimed at ensuring children can keep both parents meaningfully in their lives. Carey has always believed that children need their fathers in their lives just as much as they need their mothers – no less. He was fighting for this idea long before phrases such as "co-parenting" and "shared parenting" became popular.

A strong advocate for consensus over conflict, Carey won't avoid the just fight when reason fails. Carey helps either parent – mother or father – who is being pushed out of their children's lives by the other parent.

Carey is a founding member of Canadian Lawyers for Shared Parenting. He is a past member of the Trial Lawyers' Association of British Columbia, the American Trial Lawyers' Association, Vancouver M.E.N., and of Seattle M.E.N.. He obtained his B.A. in psychology and obtained a law degree from the University of British Columbia, where he was the acting president of the student body 1968-69 and president of his graduating class in law school 1970.

Carey was born in New York City and raised primarily in Vermont. He attended the Berklee School of Jazz and the Boston Conservatory of Music.

Carey continues to practice law today and remains staunchly dedicated to helping children keep both parents meaningfully in their lives.

You can contact Carey at http://www.divorce-for-men.com

RECOMMENDED READING

- Destructive Emotions: How Can We Overcome Them? A Scientific Dialogue with the Dalai Lama" by Daniel Goleman.

- I Don't Want to Talk About It: Overcoming the Secret Legacy of Male Depression, by Terrence Real

- The Rag and Bone Shop of the Heart: Poetry Anthology, by Robert Bly

- The Prophet, by Kahlil Gibran

- The Middle Passage: From Misery to Meaning in Midlife, by James Hollis

- The Red Pill (movie)

- The Myth of Male Power, by Warren Farrell

APPENDIX A – UNETHICAL LAWYERS ABUSE CHILDREN: BRIEF TO SPECIAL JOINT COMMITTEE OF THE CANADIAN PARLIAMENT ON CHILD CUSTODY AND ACCESS

By Carey Linde
April 27, 1998

My practice of law is restricted to Family Law, focused on helping kids see more of both parents. The vast majority of my clients are men who have lost their children. As well, I help the woman who is on rare occasions without custody see more of a child that an ex-husband is being selfish with. I try to bring the same ethical standards of approach to the best interests of the children regardless as to the gender of my client.

I've been a lawyer for 26 years, and as a single dad I raised three lovely children to adulthood.

It is the lack of ethical standards in too many family law lawyers that I want to address today. I recognize the role legislators have to play but I suggest that it is society and the legal profession itself hat has to force a higher standard of ethics into the practice of family law.

When asked how they can defend admitted criminals, defense lawyers respond with what they hope appeals to the questioner's rationality and intellect: "Everyone deserves the best defense to ensure that the Crown proves every element of its case."

Family law lawyers who play both sides against the middle can make no such appeal to intellect.

Too many family law lawyers regularly go into court on behalf of controlling, selfish parents dead set on denying the other (typically a dad) meaningful or any real role in his children's lives. These lawyers argue that the child's best interest is met by turning the father into a Disneyland dad whom the children can visit every other weekend.

All the empirical evidence from developmental psychologists- and there is a ton of it - proves that children need both parents, and after the age of three to five, particularly fathers. There is a direct correlation between a wide host of emotional, learning and social detriments that can befall children in later years and the time lost with a father.

We accept that one parent who denies meaningful access to the other parent is committing child abuse, to a lessor or greater degree. Lawyers who facilitate these selfish goals (by parents of either gender) are potential child abusers, mercenaries with a mouth for hire. It is about time society knew them for what they are. The only debate is on the degree of abuse.

A severe form of child abuse is when one parent alienates a child from the other parent. (Statistically overwhelmingly mothers more than fathers.) There should be criminal sanctions against alienating parents. Lawyers retained by an alienating parent become co-conspirators in the alienation of the child.

That such lawyers have questionable ethics can be seen by watching the same lawyer acting the next day for a parent - this time the father - seeking more time with his children. Here they hypocritically attack the position of the mother's lawyer (their own position the day before) with all the high moral reasoning and vigor they can muster. The children are mere pawns to these lawyers.

It goes without saying that there are parents who are unfit. Some children really are better off not seeing a parent sometimes. But this isn't the issue facing most courts most of the time. Rather, judges are asked to give one parent "victory" over the other parent who is only fighting for an equal role. Most parents are decent folk suffering only the hardships our corporate society inflicts on all but a few.

There are, as you know better than most, many reasons for the problems in the law of custody and access. Some are undoubtedly inherent in the human condition. Others can be worked on.

From the perspective of the child, there is one simple thing family law lawyers can do to clean up their act: stop acting against the best interests of children. Lawyers who act against children's best interests fall into one of three groups:

1. Those men and women who believe that mothers are inherently, biologically superior to men when it comes to love, affection and bonding with children. These lawyers still adhere to the discredited doctrine once known as the "maternal preference" or "tender years" doctrine, and they choose to ignore or rationalize away all the evidence to the contrary. They honestly believe that the admitted and dynamic differences between men and women translate out in court as making women superior and men inferior as parents.

Psychologist Dr. Joan Kelly, one of North America's most renowned experts in the field, in a paper delivered in 1995 entitled "The Determination of Child Custody" delivered to family law lawyers in Vancouver said: "No empirical evidence supports the distinction between primary and secondary caretaker after age five..."

And yet this committee has received briefs attempting to keep kids from "maximum" time with dads because mothers are "primary caregivers." You are being sold a bill of goods!

2. Those men and women who will argue either side of any argument as long as they get paid. This, after all, is the basic credo of most lawyers.

3. Gender feminist lawyers with a political agenda of their own that doesn't include children - at least not male children.

Just as criminal lawyers constantly get asked how they can defend criminals, the public and the media should be demanding of family lawyers how they can justify anything less than "maximizing contact between the child and each parent." These are the words of Madam Justice McLachlin of the Supreme Court of Canada in *Young vs Young 1993*.

The standard dictionary definition of 'maximum' is: "the most," or "the greatest quantity."

The high principles and standards laid out by the Supreme Court of Canada in the Young decision as to the "best interest of the child test" get eviscerated in the lower courts daily where the "every other weekend and Wed. afternoons" cookie cutter approach to access is routinely argued and applied. This fact - the enormous gulf between the stated principles of the highest court in our land and the compromising practice in the lower courts - is the biggest single obstacle to meaningful reform in this country.

Loving, caring, strong hearted men unfairly and unjustly lose their children daily in Canada as a result, among others, of the factors I've mentioned above. It also happens occasionally to women. Many see it as legal kidnapping. To understand their justifiable anger, one need only recall that society thought so ill of kidnapping that for a long time it was a capital offense in civilized societies.

A committee of parliamentarians concerned about fairness in custody and access issues has to realize that the gender-neutral divorce laws are not the problem. The problem is with the "Judicially assumed presumptions" that govern the day to day determinations of the best interest of the child test in our lower courts. These "presumptions" typically have never been put to the test of evidence, but spring from and are maintained out of gender biases still ingrained in the system.

Often challenged on this last point, I say this: Suppose fifty couples - fifty dads and fifty moms - all come into the courts on the same day. In each case both spouses are seeking an order for exclusive possession of the matrimonial home - seeking to have the other parent kicked out of the house, leaving the kids at home.

All the dads and all the moms are equally good parents. All one hundred individuals have exactly the same income and stable jobs. The kids are all around 10 to 12 years old.

If gender equity prevailed in our courts as some would lead us to believe, at the end of the court day, 25 men should be ordered out and 25 women ordered out. Half the parents left in the home with the kids should be dads and half moms. If you believe that, you believe in the tooth fairy.

What would really happen?

If these 50 cases were real ones in the courts of this Province at least, at the end of the court day the odds are that there is a reasonable chance that fifty women would be left in their homes with the kids and fifty dads expelled. This result would surprise no one. It happens every day. The odds are even stronger (almost certain) that "most" women would be left in the home with the kids.

So ... where's the fairness?

A legal profession concerned about its tarnished image can find no better place to apply disinfectant than in the area of family law.

And what can this committee do? Show moral leadership.

In 1839 the laws of England regarding custody and access were changed. Prior to that date children were the property of their fathers and stayed with them after separation. Mothers had little if any rights to see the children at all.

That injustice to children was vigorously fought by lobby groups of mothers and women. They had the support of some enlightened men. In 1839 children obtained rights to see more of mom. Now the pendulum has swung too far the other way.

It is as stupid for women's groups today to claim that this committee should pay no heed to father's groups as it would have been in 1839 for men to plead with the English Parliament to pay no attention to the mother's groups.

It is not an understatement to say that this committee would not exists but for the outright agitation of fathers in this country. And it will be children who benefit.

The organized women's movement, for all the good it has brought, gave up long ago on ideas like joint custody and shared parenting. Their silence is deafening.

Having said that, it is important that I recognize and thank all the individual women (mothers, sisters, wives and daughters) with strong feminist credentials - and even more without - who support these fathers. I call these women equity feminists, and they are the vast majority of women, whether or not most women today disavow being a feminist. I distinguish them from the gender feminists who should more properly should be called adolescent feminists. Adolescent feminists are the ones who stridently demand all the privileges and rights without any of the responsibilities. They are the teenage child wanting to borrow the car, but not willing to pay for the gas. They will never grow up into healthy adulthood.

Beware particularly these adolescent feminists who have a vested interest in victimhood and keeping the war going. How can you tell who they are? Simple! Whenever they come before you and use the word "men" in their derogatory campaign, substitute into the sentence for "men" the word "black" or "Jew", and you will see them to be the bigots they are.

You have a very difficult task ahead of you. Don't be swayed from your job by those of either gender who wish to maintain the status quo. Listen not for the feminists or the masculinists but for the humanists. Theirs's is the way out of the gender wars - men and woman putting the interests of children truly ahead of their own.

APPENDIX B – IT'S TIME TO LEGISLATE SHARED PARENTING

By Carey Linde
The Verdict Magazine
June 2006

It seems every decade of so social and legal utopians resurrect the idea of a unified family court, mandatory mediation and other assorted nostrums. The current incarnation is entitled "The Justice Review Task Force."

Its hypothesis seems to be that separating couples retain sufficient rationality to resolve their issues, but for the structural impediments in the existing legal system. There is some truth to this where both members of the couples in fact have maintained a semblance of rationality.

The problem is that many high conflict family files, particularly those involving children, all too often have one party who not only lacks rationality but typically exhibits traits of one or more personality disorders. No tinkering with the administrative structure is going to help resolve those files.

The most difficult cases are those where one parent is more or less sane, rational, and willing to compromise. But they are up against a former spouse who typically seeks to "own" the children and needs them as emotional crutches to support some psychological void in their own personality. As well, the lure of child support payments plays and inordinately destructive role in too many custody disputes. No degree of jerry rigging administrative procedures is going to help the children of that couple. For such couples, what is require is a change in the law.

Several decades ago, similar attention was given to the problem of how to avoid litigation arising out of wives suing husbands for a half interest in "the ranch" when all the family property was in the husband's name. The ultimate solution was a change in the law: a rebuttal presumption of 50/50 ownership. Litigation over property has not disappeared since then but it certainly has been lessened. A husband of a 12 your marriage sits down before his lawyer with a list of all the assets that are in his name and he is told right off the top that everything is going to go pretty much 50/50, so "save yourself the money and agreed to it and get on with other issues". The burden is now on the party claiming it should not be an even division. It took a few years but the public has a basic understanding of that principle now.

Judges and Masters are making an increasing number of equal-time-shared parenting orders. They do this both on interim applications and at trial. Various types of parenting plans resulting in approximately equal time for children with both parents are being ordered. Psychologists support it.

Many more separating parents are agreeing between themselves to shared parenting, even with children of very young years.

However, it still remains the expensive and time consuming effort that a parent seeking shared parenting has the burden to establish that it is in the best interest of the child. This typically requires Examination for Discovery, Section 15 reports (custody and access) as well as other expert opinions where the results of interim applications seeking shared parenting fail to satisfy the application and it goes on to trial. For many, trial is the only effective forum for a parent to "prove" shared parenting is in the best interest of the child.

The time has come for the Federal and Provincial legislators to place a presumption of equal-time-shared parenting in the appropriate legislation. The burden should shift to the person claiming that equal-timed-shared parenting will not work.

The author suggests that if the legislatures did with parenting schedules what they did with property a few decades ago, much litigation could be avoided, and if not avoided, simplified.

However, merely enacting a law saying there shall be a rebuttable presumption of equal-time-shared parenting will be insufficient. What many and may not constitute evidence capable of rebutting is vital and must be clarified. Otherwise, we will be no further ahead than we are with the subjective concept of "best interest of the child."

Some of the most commonly used reasons by Master and Judges to not grant equal-time-shared parenting are all, at heart, subjective. They are based, in the main, on unsubstantiated claims by the parent seeking to deny shared parenting. They are not based on any empirical evidence that the particular issue is, in and of itself, destructive of, or preventative of, or inappropriate for the amount of time that the child actually spends with both parents. These issues are such things as lack of communication between the parents, unsubstantiated claims of stress upon a child, uncorroborated allegations of abuse of a parent, or past or present conduct between parents that does not affect the children, the most commonly waved flag, "primary parent".

There is no evidence to support the proposition that a child above the age of two or three years of age will grow up a particular way determined by whether it was raised by the "primary" or so-called "secondary" parent. And yet this mantra prevails throughout the land. Legislation containing a rebuttable presumption on parenting would force the parent relying upon the concept of "primary parent" to prove that it has any evidentiary meaning.

The statutory amendments which would go some way to breaking the parenting schedule log jams cluttering up the court system would be as follows:

The Family Relations Act of B.C. shall be amended:

    a. By the addition of a new Section in Part – Child Custody, Access and Guardianship: "There shall be a rebuttable presumption of Shared Parenting. Any judgement of a court that rebuts the presumption of Shared Parenting shall contain the reasons for the rebuttal and the evidence in support of the reasons."

    b. By the addition to Section 1 (Definitions) of:

> Shared parenting means that the children of separated parents shall spend equal time with both parents.

The following factors may not be taken into consideration by a court as rebutting the presumption of Shared Parenting:

    a. The lack of communication between the parents;

    b. Allegations of stress on a child without evidence from a physician or registered psychologist;

    c. Allegations of abuse by a parent toward a child without corroborating evidence;

    d. The past or present conduct of the parents towards one another;

    e. Primary parent.

The Divorce Act of Canada shall be amended:

    a. The substitution of existing Section 16 (10) with: "There shall be a rebuttable presumption of Shared Parenting." "Any judgement of a court that rebuts the presumption of Shared Parenting shall contain reasons for the rebuttal and the evidence in support of the reasons."

    b. By addition to Section 2 (Definitions) of: Shared parenting means that the children of separated parents shall spend equal time with both parents.

Finally, a court that rebuts the presumption should state clearly the reason for doing so and the evidence upon which it is based. Too many parents leave court with no understanding as to why matters turned out the way they did. Counsel have no basis upon which to give advice as to appeal.

APPENDIX C - GENDER BIAS IN THE FAMILY COURTS OF CANADA: FACT OR FANTASY?

Presentation to Fathers Are Capable Too (F.A.C.T.)

By Gene Colman
Tuesday, March 16, 1999

What is "Gender Bias"? Is there a particular problem with gender bias in Canada's Family Courts? Is it a "fact" or is it a "fantasy" dreamed up by frustrated male litigants and their lawyers? What can we do to ameliorate what many perceive to be the injustice that is said to pervade judicial family law decision making?

Tonight, I will attempt to address some of these questions. We will be talking about gender stereotypes. We will be talking about discrimination. We will be talking about "injustice", and we will be talking about "justice". But most important of all, we will be talking about hope, fairness and our collective ability to make a difference.

Had time permitted, I would have liked to have discussed in more detail the historical development of gender bias in law and society. Did you know that British, Canadian and American law formerly gave custody pretty well automatically to fathers almost 100% of the time? Did you know that the roots of blatant maternal preference date back in the U.S. to 1830 [Helms v. Franciscus (1830), 2 Bland Ch. (Md) 544]? [See: Anne P. Mitchell: The Hypocrisy of 'Equality' in a Family Law Context, reproduced at:

http://www.backlash.com/content/gender/1995/5-may95/page15b.html. Great Britain and Canada were a little slower to grant women more rights in this area. In 1839, Britain passed legislation enabling courts to grant custody to mothers. [An Act to amend the Law relating to

the Custody of Infants, 2 & 3 Vict. (1839), c. 54 (U.K.) -
known as Lord Talfourd's Act.] By 1886 in Britain, mothers
officially obtained rights equal to those of fathers in regard
to court ordered custody. [Guardianship of Infants Act,
1886, 49 & 50 Vict., c. 27] In Canada, by the 1920's, judicial
maternal preference was clearly established. [See: Anne
Marie Delorey: Joint Legal Custody: A Reversion to
Patriarchal Power (1989), 3 CJWL 33]

Are you aware of how the media reinforces a bias against
men by perpetuating certain negative images and
stereotypes of men? [See: Armin A. Brott: Gender Bias in
the Media: The Other Side of the Story, Nieman Reports,
Winter 1994, Nieman Foundation at Harvard University,
reproduced   at:
http://www.erols.com/jkammer/nieman.htm] But we do
not have the time to engage in this fascinating historical
analysis.

I maintain that "gender bias" is indeed a reality in
Canada's courts (as well as in the other common law
jurisdictions). Tonight, I will attempt to provide some small
degree of perspective to this most pressing injustice. There
is so much to say and unfortunately, we cannot spend hours
upon hours. Let my talk this evening serve as a preliminary
introduction.

I fully recognize that by my speaking out on this topic
that I might incur the disapproval of those who may view
my remarks as "politically incorrect" and not fully in step
with my colleagues in the Canadian Bar Association Family
Law Section and elsewhere. If I dare to criticize any of our
judges, then there may be those of my colleagues at the bar
who would view my remarks with some degree of
displeasure. However, the time has come to speak out and
speak out I will!

Once judges legislate (and they do legislate, make no
mistake about that) and once judges apply stereotypes
riddled with gender biased attitudes, then they make
themselves fair game to fair analysis, fair comment and fair
criticism. I should emphasize that my firm belief is that the
very large majority of judges in Canada have no intention to

discriminate upon grounds of gender. Like society in general, they have been influenced by popularly held stereotypes and myths that have been with us, in many cases, for years and years. These stereotypes and myths have been eagerly and professionally reinforced by radical feminists and a by a media, who like many of us, have feared to question the factual basis behind these stereotypes and myths.

Most judges want to be fair and do the right thing. It is the responsibility of litigants and their legal counsel to properly present the evidence and the authorities that challenge the myths. It is my responsibility as an observer and commentator on the Canadian legal scene to raise my voice loud and clear. The emperor has no clothes! The emperor has no clothes!

Once lawyers fail to meet the needs of a significant portion of their clientele, then it is high time that someone spoke out on the needs of those who are often not adequately serviced by the legal profession. My talk here this evening consists of what I honestly believe to be fair comment. I speak only for myself. I do not necessarily reflect the views of FACT (although no doubt many of you will welcome much of what I say); I do not purport to speak for the bourgeoning non-custodial parents' movement that is very quickly gaining prominence across North America and rapidly attracting the attention of members of provincial, federal and state legislatures. I speak only for myself. If my words find favor with you, then I thank you. If my words offend some of you, then please accept my apologies. I intend to offend no one. I do, however, intend to speak frankly and from the heart while at the same time I hope that I do still maintain that degree of balance and fairness to temper or modify my commentary so that it reflects an honest pursuit of truth, academic integrity and even handed legal analysis.

A Story

Let us start with a story - a true story as I understand it. A Polish immigrant with limited English language skills went to Fredericton's Family Court to get more contact with his five-year-old daughter. He had become unemployed. Mom applied to court for custody and dad sought to increase his two weekly afternoon visits. Mom wanted to limit dad's contact with the child. Being unemployed, dad had the time, so why not? Justice Myrna Athey was reported, in the local papers, to have made the following comment on the record:

"Many fathers don't even see their children on Wednesdays, so why should this five-year-old be spending Tuesdays and Thursdays every week with her father?"

Justice Athey reduced access to each Wednesday.

It does not end there! ... When the New Brunswick Shared Parenting Association leapt to the poor man's defence and launched a complaint to the Canadian Judicial Council and publicly encouraged others who had witnessed such comments, nineteen local lawyers publicly lambasted the individuals who had spearheaded the drive. A letter from the lawyers to the local paper stated:

Ms. Jarratt's comments are troublesome for two reasons: (1) There is no factual basis offered for the grossly generalized statements made; (2) The tactic of using a complaint by another individual as an opportunity to publicly and personally malign a judge in the language used is distasteful, particularly when the judge cannot respond to such allegations.

Individuals have the benefit of a process which permits them to complain about the conduct of a member of the judiciary. Public awareness of such a process should be encouraged. Moreover, questioning the merits of legislation and lobbying government for change is an inherent right in our democratic society.

However, publicly encouraging a campaign of complaints against a judge through the media in terms used by Ms. Jarratt is, in our view, not only irresponsible, but unacceptable.

These lawyers, while they would perhaps begrudgingly concede the right of a citizen to complain to the Judicial

Council, they do not accept that gender biased comments made by a judge in open and public court should invite an equally or even greater public response. Do not the public have a right to know what goes on in our courts? Do not members of the public have the right to respond publicly when a judge pontificates openly in a public court about men in general? In our democratic system, do not citizens have the right to publicly comment on public pronouncements made by non-elected officials, by judges? Do only lawyers have the right to comment on judge's decisions but then only in academic law reviews? Should there not be a wider public debate about the key social issues that influence judicial decision making?

By the way, the complaint to the Judicial Council was predictably dismissed.

What is "Gender Bias?"

One dictionary [The New Collins Concise English Dictionary, 1982] defines "gender" as "all the members of one sex". We all know what gender means. We are referring to "men" or we are referring to "women". That's the easy part.

That same dictionary defines "bias" as follows:

" 1. mental tendency or inclination, exp. Irrational preference or prejudice."

Another definition, from that same dictionary, cites a meaning within statistics. The dictionary reads:

" 5. Statistics. A latent influence that disturbs an analysis."

The New Collins Thesaurus [1984] gives the following synonyms for "bias":

" n. 1. Bent, bigotry, favoritism, inclination, intolerance, leaning, narrow-mindedness, one-sidedness, partiality, penchant, predilection, predisposition, prejudice, proclivity, proneness, propensity, tendency, turn, unfairness. 2. Angle, cross, diagonal line, slant ~ v. 3. Distort, influence, predispose, prejudice, slant, sway, twist, warp, weight.

It is clear, I would suggest, that the emotional overtones of the word, "bias", evoke a visceral, gut reaction to the effect that "bias" is hardly a praiseworthy quality. When we accuse a legal system, a judge or a lawyer of being "gender biased", then this can be interpreted as an attack, an insult. No wonder that the Fredericton lawyers jumped to the defence of the their Family Court judge! I suggest that when a citizen simply states, in his or her pristine innocence, and when a lawyer simply states in his or her not so pristine innocence, that 'the emperor has no clothes', then the communal reaction ought to be: "My dear, let us examine our previous views to see whether or not the emperor indeed has no clothes."

Just because the word, "bias" has such negative connotations, does that mean that those who are the subject of "gender bias" or those who care deeply about the issue, should sit still and be silent? The time for polite silence has long passed. I will demonstrate this evening, through just a few examples, how the law of Canada is rising to rid itself of gender bias in some areas, while in another area, in family law, men are discriminated against, vilified and simply put down for no other reason than the fact that they are men. It is curious indeed that gender bias is being wrestled to the ground in those areas where women have historically been faced with the most invidious and objectionable discrimination. But when men are subject to equally objectionable stereotyping, then this passes as science or common sense.

I, therefore, define gender bias in the context of our legal system as follows:

"Gender Bias" is the tendency to interpret the actual facts of the case before the court through a judicial prism of favoritism to one gender over the other where such favoritism is based on prejudice, stereotyping, distortion and irrational preference. (In the worst cases of "gender bias" the actual facts are not "interpreted"; the facts are actually ignored.)

"Gender Bias" is not exemplified, I must emphasize,

where a man loses a court case. There are cases where the position advanced by a man in court is not well taken and there is ample reason for the decision to go against him. I was consulted recently by a man who had come through a long term marriage. His wife had left with him with apparently no warning and had gone to live in a basement apartment. This wife had no independent means of support. She was elderly and had been a stay at home mom during this long marriage. She had no skills and no job prospects. Where a marriage breaks down for any reason and where certain statutory criteria are met, the Divorce Act mandates that the spouse in the economically superior position shall pay spousal support. While one could argue that there should be no such thing as spousal support and that it should be the responsibility of the state to support the economically disadvantaged spouse, most would admit that spousal support is necessary and proper in these circumstances. However, the individual of whom I am speaking felt quite passionately that he was suffering from "gender bias" since he had been ordered to pay spousal support. He urged me to challenge the law. I declined. Gender bias does not mean that a man is faced with an order he does not like or does not think is fair.

Note that in my discussion of definition of "gender bias" I do not allude to the passing by Parliament or provincial legislatures of the actual laws themselves. While there is some residual bias within the black letter statutes themselves, I can say with some degree of confidence that the vast majority of the laws in Canada in 1999 are worded in gender neutral terms. The greater part of the problem lies, I suggest, with the judicial interpretation of our statutes as applied to the facts of individual cases.

I would like to quote from my esteemed colleague, lawyer Carey Linde of Vancouver, B.C. In his concise, forceful and persuasive submission to the Joint Committee [Carey Linde: "Unethical Lawyers Abuse Children", Submission to the Special Senate Commons Joint Committee on Custody and Access, www.divorce-for-men.com] Carey said this:

A committee of parliamentarians concerned about fairness in custody and access issues has to realize that the gender-neutral divorce laws are not the problem. The problem is with the "judicially assumed presumptions" that govern the day to day determinations of the best interest of the child test in our lower courts. These "presumptions" typically have never been put to the test of evidence, but spring from and are maintained out of gender biases still ingrained in the system.

On the other hand, I must admit that there appear to be statutes that although worded in a facially gender neutral manner, they really are targeted at men. A prime example of such legislation would be the Child Support Guidelines. The Guidelines fail to recognize the parenting expenditures of the non-custodial parent, who is usually the man. This problem is the subject of a Charter challenge that I currently have the privilege of conducting on behalf of a very dedicated and idealistic client. Another prime example would be the so-called Family Responsibility legislation. Legislation should not discriminate on gender grounds.

Can We Shatter the Myths?

[Many of the sources referred to here have been culled from an excellent paper by Carey Linde: A Case for Fathers and Co-parenting. This paper can be downloaded from his web site: www.divorce-for-men.com/downloads.htm. Another resource is Sanford Braver and Diane O'Connell: Divorced Dads: Shattering the Myths, Penguin Putnam, 1998.]

Myths pervade our general culture and it is therefore understandable that judges who decide real live cases may also be influenced by stereotypes. What passes as common sense one day or what passes as scientific research findings the next day, may all be shown, on more rigorous examination, to be nothing more than expressions of gender stereotyping, prejudice and bias. It is the job of lawyers and it is the job of FACT and other similar groups, to gather the evidence that is already out there and forcefully, cogently and logically challenge the "wisdom" of the past. Let us examine some of that "wisdom" of the past against the mounting volume of social science research evidence. We will see that research calls into question society's assumptions about child support, spousal support, and whether maternal custody is automatically better for children.

Myth: [with thanks to F.R.E.E., Fathers Rights Equality Exchange: Myth America - The Myth of the "Deadbeat Dad" at www.dadrights.org/myth_content.shtml] - Deadbeat dads stash money and assets in offshore investments and jet off to St. Moritz to ski the slopes with the new girlfriend, while mom and the kids languish at taxpayers' expense. $34 Billion in child support goes unpaid every year.

Reality:
- Most dads do pay their child support, in full.
- Those that don't pay:
  - don't because they haven't the means to pay;
  - still find a way to make partial payments.
- $5.8 Billion in child support was unpaid in 1992 (the last year for which figures are available).

(Authority cited: Current Population Reports P23-163 U.S. Dep't of Commerce, Census Bureau)

Myth: Sociologist, Lenore Weitzman has reported that women suffered a 73% drop in their standard of living following divorce while men experienced a 42% increase in theirs. [Lenore Weitzman: The Divorce Revolution, 1985] This study has been cited favorably in numerous American cases as well as in a number of Canadian cases such as Keast (1986), 1 R.F.L. (3) 140 (Ont. H.C.); Linton (1988), 11 R.F.L. (3d) 444, 29 E.T.R. 14, 64 O.R. (2d) 18, 49 D.L.R. (4th) 278 (Ont. H.C.); Wedgwood (1989), 74 Nfld & P.E.I.R. 198, 23 A.P.R. 198 (Nfld U.F.C.); Benson (1994), 3 R.F.L. (4 th) 291, 120 Sask. R. 17 (Sask. C.A.): Moge (1992), 43 R.F.L.(3d) 345 (S.C.C.)

Reality: For years I accepted the Weitzman study as

'truth'. But then I started to think about my own 20 years' experience as a family law lawyer. I tried to recall those situations where the man improved his economic position post separation and divorce to the woman's detriment. And guess what? I could think of precious few cases that fit the Weitzman model. The prime example where the model applies is one case that I recently took on: The husband and wife went to the same lawyer. Child support was fixed at $300.00 per month for four kids. The husband earned approximately $65,000.00; the wife earned less than $20,000. The wife paid full retail value for the husband's share in the matrimonial home. There was no spousal support. In this case, the husband had relieved himself of the mortgage payments, gotten full value for his share in the home, and was paying drastically inadequate child support. The problem here was unique to a situation where a lawyer participated in what basically amounted to perpetrating a fraud upon the wife.

There might be a few other cases that I have heard about where the husband was very wealthy and used his superior economic power to impoverish the wife through protracted litigation. But these cases are the exception - not the rule. Virtually all the cases I have seen witness the standards of living of both sides going down. For most of us, it is a struggle to maintain mortgage payments, debt payments and other responsibilities. When you add separation and divorce into the mix, the same money has to provide for two households rather than one. Common sense tells us that everyone's standard of living suffers. That is the economic reality of separation and divorce that my 20 years' experience demonstrates. Weitzman just has to be wrong!

Indeed, further studies show that at best Weitzman was innocently mistaken. At worst, - well I do not want to say.

"The problem was that Weitzman's numbers were woefully inaccurate, a conclusion shared by independent researchers, feminist researchers, and, eventually even Weitzman herself." [Cynthia A. McNeely: Lagging Behind the Times: Parenthood, Custody and Gender Bias in the

Family Court, 25 Florida State University Law Review 891 (Summer 1998)]

Respected economists whose figures were used by Weitzman in her research, found that divorced women's standards of living actually rose within five years to a figure higher than that obtained while married to their former husbands. [Id.]

Sanford Braver's book, Divorced Dads: Shattering the Myths, demonstrates that much of the research on the topic subsequent to Weitzman's fails to consider the U.S. Tax Code which, like our own, favors the single custodial parent. Like our own Child Support Guidelines, this research also fails to consider the non-custodial father's spending on the children. After making these adjustments, Braver tells us that the economic effects of divorce are similar for both genders; mother might even have a slight advantage. [Source for parts of this summary: Book Review by Cathy Young in The Detroit News, October 21, 1998, as forwarded by Nicholas J. Kovats, Freedom for Kids]

The U.S. Census Bureau has confirmed in a study that Weitzman's 73% number was wrong and inconsistent with her own information. Eventually, Weitzman herself acknowledged her study was erroneous. [Id.]

A side note: Even where one Canadian court acknowledged that the Weitzman work was flawed, it still accepted the same analysis: See Baker v. Baker (1996) 22 R.F.L. (4th) 13, 182 A.R. 41 (Alta Q.B.):

I am aware the Weitzman study has been criticized, and that further research has been done which supports the conclusion that the impact of divorce upon women is not statistically greater five years after divorce than the impact on women of the general conditions of the work force. (Faludi, Susan: "Backlash: The Undeclared War Against American Women", Anchor Books, Doubleday, 1991.) However, the Supreme Court of Canada in Moge (supra) did not rely solely on the Weitzman study to conclude that divorce support awards were impoverishing women and allowing men to become richer.

Myth: The best interests of a child normally lie with the "primary caretaker" to whom custody should normally be awarded.

Reality: "No empirical evidence supports the distinction between primary and secondary caretaker after age five, as children's greatly increased social, cognitive, and emotional maturity creates changes in the meaning of attachments and parent-child relationships to the child." (Emphasis added.) [Joan B. Kelly: The Determination of Child Custody, Children and Divorce, Vol. 4 No. 1, Spring 1994] According to Mr. Linde, data in this paper suggests that there is no distinction between primary and secondary caretaker even before the age of five.

Myth: Women suffer a legislative and practical disadvantage in Canada's family courts.

Reality: While divorce represents a loss which deprives fathers of an attachment figure and a role or identity, it also constitutes a situation where fathers are judicially and legislatively disadvantaged on the basis of gender. [Edward Kruk: Psychological and Structural Factors Contributing to the Disengagement of Noncustodial Fathers After Divorce, Family and Conciliation Courts Review, Vol. 30, No. 1, January 1992]

Myth: Men are not usually as capable of being custodial parents as are mothers.

Reality: "Fathers who have sole custody echo the complaints of mothers with sole custody. They feel overburdened, just as the mothers do, but the evidence indicates contrary to the stereotype that divorced men can rear and nurture their children competently and are equally capable of managing the responsibilities of custody, with the possible exception that the fathers have been found more effective when it comes to matters like discipline, enforcing limits, and that's particularly with boys." [Dr. Richard A. Warshak's submission to the Joint Interim Committee on Family Law for State of Missouri. Dr. Warshak is author of "The Custody Revolution - The Father Factor and the Motherhood/Mystique".]

"Park and Sawin found that fathers fed their babies as effectively and efficiently as did their spouses. They solved their feeding problems, burped and stroked, awakened and soothed appropriately and, most important, got as much milk into their babies in the allotted time as did their spouses. This rather surprising finding held true whether or not the fathers had extensive experience with babies before their own were born." [Kyle D. Pruett: The Nurturing Father, Warner Books, 1987]

"Clear support cannot be found for the belief that fathers do not have the same sensitivity as mothers do, nor the belief that fathers do not have the capacity to assume the day-to-day responsibility for child care. On the contrary, studies show that fathers can be just as sensitive and competent in care-giving as mothers. In one group of studies, researchers have compared the psychological and physiological responses of mothers and fathers to infant smiles and cries (Frodi & Lamb, 1978; see also Berman, 1980). Findings show that when given this opportunity and encouragement, fathers are just as sensitive and responsive to infants as mothers are. In another group of studies (See Parke, 1979) mothers and fathers were observed interacting with their newborn babies in the first few days after birth. During this observational session, fathers were found to be just as involved with and nurturing towards their infants (e.g., in touching, looking at, kissing, talking to). Also, fathers were found to be just as competent at feeding. They were equally likely to be able to detect infant cues, e.g., sucking, burping, and coughing, and were just as successful, as measured by the amount of milk consumed by the infant." [Graeme Russell and Norma Radin: Increased Paternal Participation, Chapter 9 in Fatherhood and Family Policy edited by Michael E. Lamb and Abraham Sagi published by Lawrence Erlbaum Associates 1983, page. 157]

"The major finding of the study was that across a variety of assessments of psychological well-being (self-esteem, anxiety, depression, problem behaviors), children (especially boys) did significantly better in the custody of their fathers. Moreover, children in father custody had the advantage of maintaining a more positive relationship with the nonresidential parent - the mother." [K. Alison Clarke-Stewart and Craig Haywood: Advantages of Father Custody and Contact For the Psychological Wellbeing of School-Age Children (1996), 17 Journal of Applied Developmental Psychology 239]

Myth: Mothers have closer bonds with children, particularly those of tender years. Children do not bond to fathers as closely as they do to their mothers.

[From the recent case of B.B. v. T.H.B., unreported, digested at [1999] O.J. No. 45 (Ont. Fam. Ct) Philp. J., 4 January 1999 at paragraph 148]: "The rule that children of tender years belong with their mother has been considered by the courts as a rule of human sense or common sense rather than a rule of law. It is only one factor to be considered with all the circumstances."

Reality: "Numerous studies have established beyond a doubt that infants form close attachment bonds with their fathers and that this occurs at the same time that they form attachments to their mothers. Although father and mother usually play different roles in their child's life, "different" does not mean more or less important." [Dr. Richard A. Warshak: The Custody Revolution - The Father Factor and the Motherhood/Mystique]

" ... a warm, involved, caring father does militate against antisocial behavior, and an inadequate father does increase the probability of delinquency. As in the case of intellectual development and social development, a father can be a predominantly positive or negative influence with regard to his children's moral development. And this runs counter to our cultural prejudice, which consistently devalues the father's contribution to his children's psychological development ... for the better part of this century, our society and it's institutions have overlooked all but the father's economic contribution to his children." [Warshak, id.]

" ... stereotypes about the nature of men, women, and children have dictated custody decisions throughout history. In earlier times, it was assumed that men, by nature, are better suited to protect and provide for children. Since

1920, it has been assumed that women, by nature, are better suited to love and care for children ... As guidelines for custody dispositions, folklore, sentiment, and stereotypes are poor substitutes for factual information." [Warshak, id.]

Myth: Upon family breakup, young children will miss their mother more than their father and therefore, young children should stay with their mother.

Reality: Many studies show that children show no particular preference for or problem with either parent staying or leaving. [Michael E. Lamb: The Role of the Father in Child Development, Whiley Press, 1976]

Children in stress or not in stress showed no apparent preference for either parent. [Id.]

There was no difference in protest following maternal or paternal departures. [Id.]

Little difference was found between infant attachment to mom or dad. [Shirley M.H. Hanson and Frederick W. Bozett: Dimensions of Fatherhood, Sage Publications, 1985]

Myth: "We all agree unequivocally that access denials form a miniscule part of our practices." [Canadian Bar Association National Family Law Section Chairperson, Heather McKay, as reported in The Lawyers Weekly, May 29, 1998: Denial of child access not the main problem: CBA, page 7]

Reality: [Excerpt from a Letter to the Editor by Gene C. Colman]:

"On the contrary, I maintain that the problem of access denial is much more widespread than it should be or my colleagues in the Family Law Section apparently believe it to be. Liberal M.P. Roger Gallaway, the chair of the Joint Committee, was quoted in the May 10 Sunday Sun as having received a submission from the Ottawa-Carleton C.A.S. to the effect that of the 900 complaints received which involved custody - access cases, 600 were shown to be unfounded or unsubstantiated. A 1991 article in the American Journal of Orthopsychiatry reported that in a survey of 220 divorcing couples, noncustodial parents reported significantly more visits with their children, as well as significantly more denial of visitation by their ex-spouses, than did custodial parents.

While I agree that more empirical studies would be helpful, in the meantime there are a significant number of Canadian noncustodial parents who are laboring against a 'stacked deck'; legislation is required now to better foster and encourage contact between children and both their parents. Unreasonable denial of access, false claims of abuse, and other tactics which deprive children of a separated/divorced parent, are significant and tragic problems that call out not only for social solutions (as correctly advocated by the C.B.A. committee), but for effective legislative remedies as well."

In a 1997 study "40% of the custodial wives reported that they had refused to let their ex-husband see the children at least once, and admitted that their reasons had nothing to do with the children's wishes or the children's safety but were somehow punitive in nature." However, the study is silent on what percentage of custodial fathers do the same. [Julie A. Fulton: "Parental Reports of Children's Post-Divorce Adjustment", Journal of Social Issues, Vol. 35, 1997, p. 133] Fifty-three percent of the non-custodial fathers claimed their ex-wives had refused to let them see their children.

In another major work on the subject:

42% of children said their mothers tried to prevent them from seeing their fathers after divorce - 16% said their fathers tried to prevent them seeing their mothers. [Glynnis Walker: Solomon's Children - Exploding the Myths of Divorce, New York: Arbor House, 1986]

How Have the Court Dealt With Gender Bias?

How have the courts dealt with gender bias? We have some very encouraging signals, including one recently from the Supreme Court of Canada, that gender bias and stereotyping is not be to be tolerated.

One level headed jurist [Justice Cecelia Johnstone of the Alberta Queen's Bench, in MacCabe v. Westlock Roman Catholic Separate School District No. 110, unreported, digested at [1998] A.J. 1053 (Alta Q.B.) 5 October 1998, Johnstone, J.] bucked precedent in a personal injury action and held that a determination of a school girl's future lost income claim should not be prejudiced by using statistical yardsticks that reinforced lower wages for women versus men. Justice Johnstone stated (I have added the emphasis):

[para469] It is entirely inappropriate that any assessment I make continues to reflect historic wage inequities. I cannot agree more with Chief Justice McEachern of the British Columbia Court of Appeal in Tucker, supra, that the courts must ensure as much as possible that the appropriate weight be given to societal trends in the labor market in order that the future loss of income properly reflects future circumstances. Where we differ is that I will not sanction the "reality" of pay inequity. The societal trend is and must embrace pay equity given our fundamental right to equality which is entrenched in the constitution. The courts have judicially recognized in tort law the historical discriminatory wage practices between males and females. The courts have endeavored to alleviate this discrimination with the use of male or female wage tables modified by either negative or positive contingencies. However, I am of the view that these approaches merely mask the problem: how can the Court embrace pay inequity between males and females? I cannot apply a flawed process which perpetuates a discriminatory practice. The application of the contingencies, although in several cases reduce the wage gap, still sanction the disparity.

[para470] A growing understanding of the extent of discriminatory wage practices and the effect of this societal inequity must lead the Court to retire an antiquated or limited judicial yardstick and embrace a more realistic, expansive measurement legally grounded in equality. Equality is now a fundamental constitutional value in Canadian society. As Chief Justice Dixon (as he then was) has noted in Canada Safeway v. Brooks, [1989] 1 S.C.R. 129, there have been profound changes in women's labor force participation. Since Brooks there has been even greater accommodation of the parental needs of working

women. The Court cannot sanction future forecasting if it perpetuates the historic wage disparity between men and women. Accordingly, if there is a disparity between the male and female statistics in the employment category I have determined for the Plaintiff the male statistics shall be used, subject to the relevant contingencies. Once again if the contingencies are gender specific, then the contingencies applicable to males shall be used except in the case of life expectancy, for obvious reasons.

What Justice Johnstone does in this case is this - she jettisons factually incorrect stereotypes with respect to women's position in the modern day labor market. Just because old statistical projections said that women historically earned less than men, this is not sufficient justification, in an era of pay equity and Charter equality, to award a woman less for the future wage loss component of her personal injury damages. Justice Johnstone is quite correctly telling us that outmoded societal biases with respect to women's wages are inconsistent with equality before the law. Her Honour states: "I cannot apply a flawed process which perpetuates a discriminatory practice." Could such a sentiment ... could such a noble and just sentiment be applied in child custody law?

Justice Johnstone states: "As Chief Justice Dixon (as he then was) has noted in Canada Safeway v. Brooks, [1989] 1 S.C.R. 129, there have been profound changes in women's labor force participation. Since Brooks there has been even greater accommodation of the parental needs of working women. The Court cannot sanction future forecasting if it perpetuates the historic wage disparity between men and women." " Profound changes in women's labor force participation" - think about that concept for a moment. It is quite true. We all know that from our everyday experience. It makes sense, doesn't it? There have been societal changes in the way women work in society, in their opportunities for advancement, in the level of their wages. In most places, it is recognized as discriminatory if not illegal to pay a woman less for the same job that a man does. And that is as it should be!

So let us now turn to Justice John Goodearle in Banks v. Banks, [unreported, 19 December 1986, digested at [1987] W.D.F.L. 147, 2 A.C.W.S. (3d) 436, 9 F.L.R.R. 132 (Ont. U.F.C)]. This was the first Ontario case under the 1985 amendments to the Divorce Act where joint custody was imposed over mom's objections. Decided in December 1986, the case is the family law parallel to the above personal injury damages case. But first, let us note what subsection 16(10) of the Divorce Act states. It was added in the 1985 amendments and is popularly known as the "friendly parent" provision.

Justice Goodearle begins the most important part of his joint custody decision by stating [pp. 23-24]:

Section 16.(10) is new and of significant help in the case at bar. It reads:

16(10) In making an order under this section, the court shall give effect to the principle that a child of the marriage should have as much contact with each spouse as is consistent with the best interests of the child and, for that purpose, shall take into consideration the willingness of the person for whom custody is sought to facilitate such contact."

The judge then goes on to discuss the new era in childcare. He states:

Subsection (4), and (10) of section 16 may well ordain the dawning of a new era in the sharing of child raising responsibilities by divorcing parents. For it seems that the Parliament of Canada, in proclaiming these sections into law, has acceded to the reality of some rather monumental changes in our modern day socioeconomic fabric. Most notably, that the modern day woman has broadened her range of vocations enormously and as well her appetite for participation in the work force after child birth. This is in contrast to the woman of yesteryear who participated in a traditional marriage which recognized her as the nurturer and homemaker and her husband as the bread-winner. Such a sociological change has of course quite obviously made modern day working women much less available to her historically traditional duties in child raising and, by nature social evolution, fathers have sprung into the breach and now participate more and more in the child's daily activities and raising which of course includes disciplining and guidance.

Just as Justice Johnstone recognized a new social reality in 1998, some twelve years earlier Justice Goodearle recognized the new social reality in childcare and the impact that could have on court decisions with respect to the role of fathers. Would that more judges take notice of Justice Goodearle's comments!

Justice Goodearle also quoted extensively from an excellent 1985 article that had been published in the Reports of Family Law [Judith P. Ryan: Joint Custody in Canada: Time for a Second Look, (1985) 49 R.F.L. (2d) 119]. That article demolished the stereotypes about women and men in the workforce, about the importance of fathers to children's development, about the pain and dislocation experienced by sole custody children, etc. etc. The judge relied on the author's reporting of the relevant social science research. Depending on the judge or the assessor, perhaps there is something to be side for bringing forward some of the various studies that cast doubt on widely held stereotypes and misconceptions.

The Ontario Court of Appeal has also struck a great blow against gender bias's first cousin, gender stereotyping. Indeed, when we stereotype a group based upon preconceived notions, we tend to ignore the actual evidence staring us in the face. How many men have been looked at by judges and by lawyers as simply 'another man' bellyaching about "access". People fail to consider the actual facts before them. "Oh, you're just a man; you don't have a chance of succeeding in court." Well, the Ontario Court of Appeal has issued the wakeup call.

That court recently had occasion to review a trial judge's award of $120,000.00 to an autoworker - supervisor for wrongful dismissal [Bannister v. General Motors of Canada Ltd., (1998), 40 O.R. (3d) 577, 164 D.L.R. (4th) 325, 112 O.A.C. 188]. The plaintiff (GM supervisor) had sexually harassed a number of his female workers and was, I would suggest, quite properly sacked. The appellate court sensibly rejected the plaintiff's "rough environment" argument. The supervisor had argued that the GM plant is a rough place where rough language and sexually suggestive banter is common place. Justice Carthy felt that the trial judge's reasons demonstrated "a complete lack of appreciation of the modern concept of equality of the sexes. " Basically, what the Court of Appeal is saying here (and it has been said in other cases as well) is that abuse and sexual innuendo are not acceptable in the workplace. In other words, in my view, the Court of Appeal is striking a needed blow in favor of gender equality.

The cases tell us that the workplace must not be a source of any kind of gender discrimination; sexual harassment is a particularly invidious expression of discrimination and it will not be countenanced under any circumstances. And, just to review Justice Johnstone's precedent setting decision, if you are disabled from working, then calculation of your lost income must be measured using statistics that are not loaded against you solely because you are female. Your gender should not cause you to suffer discrimination when assessing damages for loss of future income. All of this makes eminently good sense. It is consistent with the Charter and it probably strikes a responsive chord amongst most lawyers and judges. Who would, in their right mind, argue against such a fair minded approach?

Our highest court, the Supreme Court of Canada, has recently rendered a decision that has sparked unprecedented controversy across the land and has led to calls for the dismissal of an eminent appeal justice from Alberta and of Madam Justice L'Heureux-Dubé of the Supreme Court [R. v. Ewanchuk, unreported, digested at [1999] S.C.J. No. 10, 25 February 1999]. Briefly, the Supreme Court of Canada was hearing an appeal of a sexual assault acquittal in the Alberta trial court that was upheld by the Alberta Court of Appeal. The legal issue in the case was whether the complainant had consented, as consent is understood by the Criminal Code. A finding of an absence of consent should have been enough to send the case back for trial, however the Supreme Court of Canada convicted the accused. Where the case becomes interesting for those concerned with gender bias and stereotyping is the additional judgment proffered by Madam Justice L'Heureux-Dubé.

Madam Justice L'Heureux-Dubé states [at para 82]:

This case is not about consent, since none was given. It is about myths and stereotypes..."

The judge then goes on to quote an author who summarizes the various myths of rape (although this case was not a rape case). She then launched into a particularly vicious personal attack on Alberta Court of Appeal Justice McClung. She criticized McClung for his references to the complainant's manner of dress and her living arrangements with her boyfriend and others.

Madam Justice L'Heureux-Dubé then stated [at para 89]:

These comments made by an appellate judge help reinforce the myth that under such circumstances, either the complainant is less worthy of belief, she invited the sexual assault, or her sexual experience signals probable consent to further sexual activity.

Reference was also made to various other comments by Justice McClung that provoked harsh criticism from Justice L'Heureux-Dubé. Each of the gender stereotypes trumpeted by the Alberta justice were demolished by Justice L'Heureux-Dubé. She states [at para 95]:

Complainants should be able to rely on a system free from myths and stereotypes, and on a judiciary whose impartiality is not compromised by these biased assumptions. The Code was amended in 1983 and in 1992 to eradicate reliance on those assumptions; they should not be permitted to resurface through stereotypes reflected in the reasons of the majority of the Court of Appeal. It is part of the role of this Court to denounce this kind of language, unfortunately still used today, which not only perpetuates archaic myths and stereotypes about the nature of sexual assaults but also ignores the law.

Madam Justice McLachlin wrote a brief concurring

opinion. She stated [at para 103]:

I also agree with Justice L'Heureux-Dubé that stereotypical assumptions lie at the heart of what went wrong in this case. ... On appeal, the idea also surfaced that if a woman is not modestly dressed, she is deemed to consent. Such stereotypical assumptions find their roots in many cultures, including our own. They no longer, however, find a place in Canadian law.

Justice Minister Anne McLellan was reported [National Post, 26 February 1999] to have praised the court for " eradicating stereotypes ... that may give women pause in how they think they will be understood by the courts of this country." On the other hand, eminent criminal law lawyer, Edward Greenspan defended the independence of the judiciary [National Post, 2 March 1999] and he defended Justice McClung from the highly personal attack launched by Justice L'Heureux-Dubé. Greenspan bemoaned how politics has taken over issues surrounding sexual assault. He stated:

It is clear that the feminist influence has amounted to intimidation, posing a potential danger to the independence of the judiciary. ... Feminists have entrenched their ideology in the Supreme Court of Canada and have put all contrary views beyond the pale.

I agree with Greenspan and I agree with all those other brave individuals who have come to the defence of Justice McClung's right to deliver an appellate judgment without being subject to a personal attack by the Supremes. I particularly agree with Greenspan when he notes that "feminist influence has amounted to intimidation". The intimidation problem is certainly not restricted to criminal law.

However, as someone who is particularly concerned with gender bias within the family court system, I see in the judgments of L'Heureux-Dubé and MacLaughlin great opportunity. The judges themselves are attacking stereotypical assumptions. I suspect that they did not appreciate the full impact of their words. We are told that eradicating stereotypes is an important task to accomplish. I agree! Let us eradicate all stereotypes! Can any even handed and open minded jurist in this country argue that these principles should apply only to sexual assault cases? Can a judge seriously maintain that Justice L'Heureux-Dubé's admonitions with respect to gender stereotyping can apply only to women but not to men? Should not these important and just principles be applied across the board? And should not such across the board application include such areas as child custody law and child support law? Are we only going to judge 'on the evidence' free from stereotypes when it comes to sexual assault, but when we talk of the importance of having fathers intimately involved in their children's lives shall we permit "myths and stereotypes" to defeat a father's claim to parent his children in a normal fashion?

"Complainants should be able to rely on a system free from myths and stereotypes, and on a judiciary whose impartiality is not compromised by these biased assumptions." - Does this judicial pronouncement pertain only to rape and sexual assault? Is it permissible to assume the worst of men because they are men?

"You dead beat dad! You have not paid your support for three months! I'm certainly not going to order Family Responsibility to refrain from suspending your driver's license, buster! "

"But Your Honour, if you will turn to page two of my affidavit, you will see that I lost my job three months ago and I have been caring full time for my elderly father who has been diagnosed with a terrible life threatening disease. And I need my license to get to get back to work so that I can pay some child support, pay my rent and buy food."

"I know a dead beat when I see one. I don't need to read your affidavit. Next case."

Is There a Particular Problem with Gender Bias in Canada's Family Courts?

Is there a particular problem with gender bias in Canada's Family Courts? I believe that there is. We certainly need proper statistical studies. We need research. Where are the dedicated graduate students of sociology, psychology and law who have not been poisoned and co-opted by politically popular anti male feminism? We need you. Where are you?

I know this: Many of my colleagues openly admit to telling their male clients, "It is not a good time to be a man in the courts of Canada these days." We say this because we know from admittedly subjective experience that to succeed as a man in court, it is much more difficult than if you are a woman. That is the reality.

Permit me to quote from the Report of the Special Joint Senate Commons Committee on Child Custody and Access [For the Sake of the Children, December 1998]. Toronto lawyer Michael Day is quoted at page 15:

When I go to court with a male client who is looking for custody, it's always an uphill battle. I always have to have a special fact situation in order to have a good chance at getting custody.

Toronto psychologist and custody assessor, Dr. Marty McKay testified [page 16]:

My finding is that there are a lot of nurturing fathers out there. I've had some women tell me they don't care how the assessment turns out because they are going to get custody of the children anyway "because they always give custody to the woman".

The Report itself noted some of the more recent statistics from Statistics Canada [page 4]:

"[M]ost children (86%) lived with their mother after separation. Only 7% lived with their father, about 6% lived under a joint custody arrangement, and the remaining (less than 1%) lived under another type of custody agreement."

These percentages are consistent with a 1989 study conducted for the Massachusetts Supreme Judicial Court on Gender Bias [Gender Bias Study of the Court System in Massachusetts (1989) reprinted in 24 New. Eng. L. Rev. 745 and cited in Cynthia A. McNeely: Lagging Behind the Times: Parenthood, Custody and Gender Bias in the Family Court, 25 Florida State University Law Review 891 (Summer 1998)]. A proper interpretation of the data revealed the following analysis:

- Mothers get primary residential custody 93.4% of the time in divorces.
- Fathers in divorce get primary residential custody only 2.5% of the time.
- Fathers in divorce get joint physical custody only 4% of the time.
- Fathers in divorce get primary or joint physical custody less than 7% of the time.
- Where fathers actively seek custody, they receive primary residency in less than one out of three cases (29%), and joint physical residency in less than half (46%).

These statistics fly in the face of the common feminist wisdom that fathers who seek custody in court more often than not succeed. This specious and false allegation is thoroughly demolished in Cynthia McNeely's article [Section III].

The plain fact of the matter is this - in order for a man to succeed in maintaining a decent relationship with his kids (and by decent I mean in terms of time with the kids and even some responsibility for major issues affecting the lives of the children), he has to be what I call, "super dad". Being just "normal dad" will not suffice. Dad has to prove to the court that he is one of those exceptional fathers who is ever so keenly attuned to all of the kids' needs. He knows their shoe sizes; he has a strong relationship with each and every teacher since kindergarten; he bakes cookies with the kids; he is a master chef; he keeps an immaculate house; he has read all of the latest child rearing books at Chapters ... at least twice; he has a veritable retinue of witnesses to attest to his superior child care abilities and his best witness is a social worker - perhaps the present or former dean of University of Toronto's Social Work faculty.

Let us not forget the often sordid role of custody-access assessors. There was an excellent article by Donna Laframboise in the National Post on January 30, 1999. She described three cases where assessors had relied on false information, faulty assumptions and in one case it was clear that the assessor proceeded from the assumption that children normally should be with their mother. The complaint routes appeared to be inadequate and ineffective, to say the least. But should we expect any more balance from assessors than we currently do from judges and lawyers? They are all part of the problem.

Is there a gender bias problem in Canada's Family Courts? When I was preparing this talk, I sent out an e-mail through Nick Kovats' educational e-mail service (which by the way is one of the best ways to keep up to date on recent developments on matters of concern to non-custodial parents across North America). I announced that I was doing a talk and some legal writing on gender bias and I invited input from those who had felt that they had experienced gender bias in our family courts. The response was gratifying, yet depressing. I received stories from across North America. Gender bias has touched many; that is clear. ... I heard from southwestern Ontario, from a dad whose family had been literally ripped apart because mom knew that the Guidelines would net her more money if she could just get that 21-year-old son who had been living with his girlfriend back into her house and back into school.

I heard from a dad in Quebec whose custody claim was refused because he did not have a job.

I heard about scores of dads (and some moms) who had been falsely accused of sexually abusing their children decades after the alleged abuse had allegedly occurred. The police and crown lawyers simply assumed that the allegations must be true and have laid many charges, some of which have been thrown out of court; many claim to have been wrongly convicted and unfortunately languish in jail to this day.

I heard from a dad in Saskatchewan who had faced 11 false charges instigated by his wife. The crown prosecuted each time even though the court threw out all of the charges. As soon as his custody trial was over, he was arrested yet again and that charge was thrown out too.

One very remarkable story came from here in Toronto. Mom kidnapped the child to South America. After the greater part of the year, the child was returned under the

Hague Convention and then dad had to slug it out at 393 University [the Court House in Toronto]. Dad was told by many, including judges, that the abduction by mom would play no part in a determination of custody! Can you imagine what part a dad's abduction would play in the court's determination?

My informant wrote as follows:

[name deleted], the social worker for the Children's Lawyer, during one of my seemingly endless meetings with them, got really angry at me when I suggested there may be some bias in the court system. Her words: "You should consider yourself lucky, Mr. X, after all, it is the policy of the government of Ontario that children stay with their mothers". When my journalist's alarms started sounding at the utterance of the word "policy", I asked her, very softly, to tell me where that policy could be found. She stammered and said: "Well, it's more of a general philosophy than a policy".

I heard from heartbroken grandparents in Alberta. Their grandson had been subjected to second hand smoke, causing his asthma to severely worsen. When dad took court action, backed by medical experts and private investigators' pictures of mom and her boyfriend smoking in the car with the boy, the female judge decided that the application was nothing more than the father trying to drive a wedge between mom and the boy and then ordered dad to pay $750.00 in costs. The grandparents close their letter to me with this: "We can assure you that if the genders in this case were reversed the father would probably have little more than supervised access."

There was a troubling news article that came across my desk [Paul McKie, The Canadian Press, printed in the National Post, February 24, 1999]. A mother who was displeased with a custody order tried to hire a contract killer to dispose of her husband. She received a sentence of only two and one half years. But that was not the worst of it. The judge, as it is reported in this article, commented that there were no psychological assessments before him to suggest that husband had abused her during the marriage.

The implication clearly is this: Had she believed that the husband abused her, she would have been justified in planning a cold, calculated murder and the sentence would have been less. Make no mistake please about what I am saying. Abuse is not excusable under any circumstances. But to imply that the belief that one is abused somehow might justify murder or a lesser sentence, certainly smacks of an invitation to all women who are pursuing a custody claim to claim abuse. The mere claim or belief that one is abused may be sufficient to obtain a tactical advantage.

Abuse allegations are very effective ways to have a husband removed and a non-contact with the children (or restraining order) put in place. I have found that a number of Provincial Division judges grant such orders without there being any notice to the father. I heard from a father in Edmonton - a heartbreaking and heartrending story. Time doesn't permit me to read his entire two-page single spaced e-mail. Let me tell you, briefly, that false abuse allegations were hurled at him, even though he and the children were the ones who were beaten. He was turfed from his home by the police enforcing an ex-parte order. Solid physical evidence of the physical abuse (let alone emotional abuse) against the children by the mother is ignored by child welfare authorities who see dad's complaints as simply part of his matrimonial case. How many men have been faced with similar brush offs by Children's Aid but when the mother complains, a full-scale investigation is launched during which lengthy period dad's time with the children is simply cancelled. In the Edmonton father's case, his daughter ran away to him but no one listens. Let me relate to you just a few quotes from this father's e-mail to me:

The whole system is bias[ed]. Women can say and do what they want and the fathers pay for it. This is not right. All I want is what is fair, that is all any good father wants. How can it be that a woman can cry abuse and it is so, but when a man has proof of a women actually doing it, that there is never enough proof.

I have never been told that they would not grant me anything, except from my ex lawyer who said I would never win a custody issue because I was a man, and that the law sees that women are more nurturing, well not in this case, I was always the one there for them for everything, not my wife. I have had the worst look from a woman judge as she entered the court room, like she already hated the fact that I even dare try for my children. This was when I was on my own after losing my first lawyer because of lack of money.

What I'm trying to say is, the law needs to look deeper into the family, to see what is really going on before they just grant the children like objects, to the women.

Yes, gender bias is a reality in Canada's courts - and especially in the family courts. Many witnesses poured out their hearts to the Special Joint Committee. Some of that testimony comes through in the Joint Committee Report; more of it was posted on the internet. In my own practice, I see my clients being subjected to gender bias. I see it when I observe other cases as I sit in court waiting for my case to be called and I hear about it from some of my colleagues. I hear it from many of you when you talk to me at the conclusion of my presentations and when you call me on the phone for some quick guidance as to how to handle your cases. Enough is enough! Injustice, no matter where it is found, should not be permitted to plague our legal system. I am not talking here about doing anything against women. We have no quarrel with women as a group. All we want is for judges, assessors and lawyers to deal with family law issues absent any prejudice, bias or ill-conceived presumptions about what "men" can do or cannot do.

What Can We Do To Ameliorate the Injustice?

What can we do to ameliorate the injustice? What can we do to sensitize judges, lawyers, social workers, assessors, the general public, to the reality of gender bias against men in the family courts of Canada?

As recently as a few days ago, the National Post reported [National Post, Saturday, March 13, 1999] that the National Shared Parenting Association is filing a complaint against all nine justices of the Supreme of Canada. The NSPA's executive director, Danny Guspie, was quoted:

"We feel public debate has opened up and we're attempting to raise the level of the public debate to take a look at what's going on with the judiciary."

This complaint has as much chance of succeeding before the Judicial Council as does ... [well you can fill that in]. Public education is much more important. It is essential to bring to the attention of the public in a very reasoned, calm and sensible way, just what is really going on in the courts of Canada. There is ample evidence. Just turn to the law reports, to the reported cases. For example, in my Child Support Guidelines articles [see my web site as well as Gene C. Colman: Guidelines' Undue Hardship Produces Conflicting Decisions, Money & Family Law, Vol. 13, No. 7, July 1998, page 53; Gene C. Colman: B.C. Court of Appeal Declines to Vary Child Support under the Child Support Guidelines, Money & Family Law, Vol. 13, No. 10, October 1998, page 75;], I point out how men and women similarly situated are treated quite differently. Likewise, in the area of child custody law, there are many examples of how men are similarly discriminated against on the grounds of gender. Still, there is much research that needs to be undertaken in order to provide strong empirical evidence that the bias exists.

I would like to see a chair established at a prestigious law school to foster research into what might be called "men's issues" but are really gender equality and "people" issues.

I would like to see more lawyers do more than simply tell their male clients - forget it. You are a man and you cannot possibly succeed. This self-defeatist outlook feeds into the stereotypes and perpetuates injustice. A lawyer must properly interview a client and see if he has the requisite fact situation that would justify pursuing matters whether through patient negotiation or through court action. Do not just assume defeat based on gender!

I would like to see a little more objectivity from my colleagues at the bar. We only hear about so-called "women's issues" and how we do not need legislative reform, how access denial is not a problem, and on and on. There is a very large constituency of clients out there who are getting the shaft because lawyers are simply not taking leadership positions when it comes to promoting gender equality and gender fairness.

I would like to see organizations like FACT and the National Shared Parenting Association keep up the struggle for gender equality within our family courts. But advance your cause with reason, patience, cogent reasonable argument and of course, suitable political lobbying.

I would like to see Senator Anne Cools cloned about 200 times over and have 150 of those clones elected to the House of Commons and 50 of them placed in the Senate. Or, how about this one? Anne Cools for Prime Minister!

I would like the media to more objectively report those issues that are important to children and to families. What sort of issues require coverage and explanation to the Canadian public? Let's try some of these: Denial of access, violence against men by their wives or partners, impoverishment of men due to impossible support awards that in some cases leave men with not even enough to pay rent and buy food, the failure of judges to read motion materials and simply deciding custody and access issues based upon assumptions, presumptions and stereotypes, and the list could go on and on.

It is time to let the Canadian public know that men facing separation and divorce are not being dealt with fairly. And if men are not being treated fairly, that means that their children are likewise suffering. But while we are so concerned with such issues, let us not forget that there are many women, particularly poor women and native women who likewise quite often are not being treated well by the courts, particularly in the child welfare field. There are women who are married to very wealthy individuals; these rich guys tend to abuse the court system with their high-priced counsel in order to pound their wives into submission. All those women deserve our support because justice, fairness and equity should cut across gender lines.

There was a time when women as a group were not being treated fairly; that was wrong and it has now been largely remedied. But the pendulum has swung too far in the opposite direction. Now it is men who face discrimination in the family courts. Court cases must be decided upon the real evidence and not on myths. I call upon all those involved in our legal system to meet the challenge. Changes can be made but we require a significant shift in attitudes.

Groups like FACT have a key role to play in the struggle to achieve true gender equality in our courts. The skill with which you present your positions to the public and to policymakers will help to determine whether or not true gender equality and justice for Canadian families will be achieved.

I would just like to close now with another quote from that father in Edmonton. His words are from the heart. It is the task of those who truly care, to take positive and resolute action in order to transform the heartfelt words from Edmonton into attitudinal change and therefore into enlightened, just public policy. That father states:

The lies that women get away with about Fathers must stop! The courts must see who is the better parent, for the children, and not just because that parent is a woman. After all, it is what's best for our children and the children of the future, that we all get together and make our laws fair for women and men, mothers and fathers, but mainly for our Sons   and   Daughters.

APPENDIX D – THE EVOLUTION, CURRENT STATUS AND FUTURE OF THE BEST INTERESTS OF THE CHILD PRINCIPLE IN THE PROTECTION OF CHILDREN'S RIGHTS

Speech by Senator Anne Cools
Delivered Nov. 25, 2015, Dr. Janusz Korczak Lecture Series, University of British Columbia.

My friends, my subject is the best interests of the child. By our Constitution, children's causes are vested not in our federal jurisdiction, but in the provinces. The 1914 Ontario Children's Protection Act, section 22.(3), said:

> *Where it appears to the Judge that the public interest and the interest of the child will be best served thereby, an order may be made for the return of the child to its parents or friends, or the Judge may place such child under the guardianship of the children's aid society or of an industrial school.*[1]

Note the likeness to the phrase *the best interests of the child* in many provincial child protection and welfare statutes. Federally, there are only two statutes about children, the Divorce Act and the Youth Criminal Justice Act, formerly the Young Offenders Act, formerly the Juvenile Delinquents Act, born of the late nineteenth century genesis in child welfare. The 1929 Juvenile Delinquents Act's legal conceptual framework was the welfare of the child and the *parens patriae*. These saw delinquency not as an offence, out as a condition in the child needing parental care and guidance. This Act's section 3.(2) said:

> *Where a child is adjudged to have committed a delinquency he shall*

---

[1] The Children's Protection Act, RSO 1914, C 231, s 22.(3), p. 3098

be dealt with, not as an offender, but as one in a condition of
delinquency and therefore requiring help and guidance and proper
supervision.[2]

From this grew the juvenile courts and, later, the family courts.

My friends, in Canada until 1968, divorce was difficult, costly and rare. They proceeded by the old British Divorce and Matrimonial Causes Act in our provinces, except Quebec and Newfoundland, where they moved as individual private bills in parliament. Begun as private bill petitions in the Senate, these individual divorce bills were debated and voted there. Then, without amendment, they were voted in the House of Commons, then given Royal Assent by the Governor General. Canada enacted its first federal Divorce Act in 1968. In 1984, the phrase *the best interests of the child* [3]and its conceptual framework were proposed for the Divorce Act by Liberal Justice Minister Mark MacGuigan. His brainchild, he offered it in his paper, *Divorce Law in Canada: Proposals for Change.* A legal scholar, he was Windsor University's Dean of Law, onetime University of Toronto law professor, and later, judge of the Federal Court of Canada His divorce Bill C-10 died when parliament dissolved for the September 4 federal election. The new Conservative Government's Justice Minister, John Crosbie, reworked it, and introduced· his own Bill C-4 7. This retained MacGuigan's best interests of the child legal framework, based in the *parens patriae* and welfare of the child doctrines. In 1986, we enacted Bill C-47 as the current Divorce Act.

My friends, the origin and pedigree of this enduring phrase, *the best interests of the child,* are not well known nor understood, for many reasons, including the now stilled late

---

[2] The Juvenile Delinquents Act, 1929, Statutes of Canada 1929, c46, s3.(2), pp.3

[3] Bill C-IO, An Act to amend the Divorce Act, 2 Sess, 32 Pari, 1984, s'10, p. 7 (first reading on January 19 1984)

1980s-1990s *gender feminism* that overtook *equality feminism*.

The former held that women are morally superior to men and that men are morally inferior to women and even morally defective. It held that moral and humane behaviour are gendered traits, that goodness and virtue are female, and that aggression, violence, and evil are male, all despite compelling evidence of gender parity and symmetry in violence. Domestic violence was then falsely framed as violence against women. All this disfigured criminal law application in physical and sexual assault cases, and divorce law cases in child custody and access, and child and spousal support. In divorce, this meant that mothers should have primary and greater parenting rights than fathers. Their lawyers held that domestic violence cases should be decided by "women's credibility," that, since women are truth tellers, their physical and sexual assault accusations against their male partners should be treated as findings of guilt. Those years saw a plethora of false accusations in divorce and child custody proceedings. It was a heart of darkness, soul destroying for fathers, their mothers and the women in their lives. In the 1994 Ontario case, *D.B. v. Children's Aid Society of Durham Region*, Justice William Somers said about a witness, at paragraph 75:

> *Ms. Chisholm indicated that the experience has been for some time that sexual assault allegations made by a mother against a father in custody disputes are very prevalent nowadays and indeed have become what she called "the weapon of* choice"[4].

My friends, this feminist privilege found help in the then Liberal Justice Minister's 1997 Bill. C-41 that amended Minister Crosbie's Divorce Act which, by *the best interests of the child* conceptual framework, had embraced gender equality in parenting and home life. Bill C-41 set out to repeal the 1986 Divorce Act's financial equality section

---

[4] Ontario Court of Justice (General Division), B(D) and B(R) and B(M) v. Children's Aid Society of Durham Region and Marion Van Den Boomen, [1994] O.J. No. 643, 46 A.C.W.S. (3d) 800, Action No. 20962/87, March 23, 1994, Justice Somers., p. 19, paragraph 75

15.(8), that had enacted shared financial obligations for both mothers and fathers, to support their children. It said:

> *An order made under this section that provides for the support of the child of the marriage should*
>
> *a) recognize that the spouses have a joint financial obligation to maintain the child; and*
>
> *b) apportion that obligation between the spouses according to their relative abilities to contribute to the performance of the obligation[5].*

Shared obligations were key to the child-centred gender equal 1986 Crosbie Divorce Act federal reforms. These followed the 1970s provincial family law reforms that enacted joint and shared property ownership of the matrimonial home and assets. The provinces had decreed shared marriage property. The federal divorce law followed, enacting shared financial and affectionate care of the marriage's children. These 1986 Crosbie Divorce Act reforms also spoke to wives' financial dependence on husbands. Section IS.2(6)(d), *Objectives of spousal support order,* decreed that support payments must:

> *in so far as practicable, promote the economic self-sufficiency of each spouse within a reasonable period of time[6].*

Another 1986 Divorce Act equality reform was the *friendly parent rule,* section 16.(10) that said:

> *In making an order under this section, the court shall give effect to the principle that a child of the marriage should have as much contact with each spouse as is consistent with the best interests of the child and, for that purpose, shall take into consideration the willingness of the person for whom custody is sought to facilitate such contact[7].*

---

[5] Divorce Act, 1986, R.S.C 1985, c.3 (2 Supp.), s. 15.(8), pp. 10 - 11

[6] Divorce Act, 1986, R.S.C 1985, c.3 (2 Supp.), s. 15.2(6)(d), p. 14 as it appeared on October 15, 2015.

[7] Divorce Act, 1986, R.S.C 1985, c.3 (2 Supp.), s. 16.(10), p. 12

In 2003, the then Liberal Justice Minister's Bill C-22 tried to repeal this *friendly parent rule*. We buried it. It did not become law.

My friends, forged in the *parens patriae* doctrine by which the Sovereign Queen, the supreme guardian of children, and her superior court judges, owe children the high duty of decisions in their best interests, the child-centred Crosbie Divorce Act held great promise for balance, fairness, and equilibrium in divorce. Sadly, later amendments to this Act, mainly Bill C-41, set out to defeat these reforms. It repealed the Divorce Act's gender equality child support sections, and replaced them with the new Federal Child Support Guidelines. These, enacted as the Act's regulations, decreed that child support payment amounts would be calculated solely on the income of non-custodial parents, mostly fathers, and paid to custodial parents, mostly mothers.

These calculated amounts do not factor in the custodial parents' income. Justice lawyers tried to convince senators that the custodial parent's financial contribution was assumed. Feigning the gender equality of the repealed child support section, the Federal Child Support Guidelines were enacted as the Divorce Act section 26.1 (2), that:

> *The guidelines shall be based on the principle that spouses have a joint financial obligation to maintain the children of the marriage in accordance with their relative abilities to contribute to the performance of that obligation*[8].

Sounds the same as the repealed section, but is not.

As regulations, meaning *delegated or subordinated legislation* decided by the Minister, these Guidelines launched the legal pre-eminence of the financial over the affectionate duties of parents to children. These regulated and dictated quantums undermined *judicial independence*, and the judges' duties to children in child support decisions. Bill C-41's other Divorce Act change then decreed the court's duty to stay

---

[8] Divorce Act, 1986, RS.C 1985, c.3 (2 Supp.), s. 26.1 (2), p. 31 as it appeared op. October 15,2015.

the divorce if the parents had not made reasonable child support arrangements for the children. So amended, the Divorce Act, section 11.(I)(b), says:

In a divorce proceeding, it is the duty of the court...

(b) to satisfy itself that reasonable arrangements have been made for the support of any children of the marriage, having regard to the applicable guidelines, and, if such arrangements have not been made, to stay the granting of the divorce until such arrangements are made; . . .[9]

No reasonable child support arrangements, no divorce. This section decrees no equal court duty to stay the divorce if the parents have not made reasonable arrangements for parenting the children. The court's power in the financial is more weighted than the affectionate. The Department lawyers said that these changes were needed for uniformity in child support payments. Very odd, this uniform child. The elevation of the parental financial duties over the affectionate is a strange beast. It has no place in *the best interests of the child*, the Divorce Act decision framework. This was enhanced by the Income Tax Act change that ended the regime whereby the income tax on child support was paid by the lower income custodial parent recipient, mostly women. Now the higher income, non-custodial parent, mostly men, would pay it. Some hailed this divorce children's financial loss as a windfall to the public purse.

Tonight I laud the late Mark MacGuigan, who enshrined *the best interests of the child* as the Divorce Act's legal-judicial framework. For him, the first of the child's best interests is its interest in its own relationship with both parents, both mother and father. He set out to effect and actuate shared parenting by enlisting the legal-judicial conceptual framework the best interests of the child as the standard for judges' decisions. By this, the Divorce Act vested Canada's children as persons, separate from their parents, with rights

---

[9] Divorce Act, 1986, R.S.C 1985, c.3 (2nd SUpp.), s. 11.(1), p. 9 as it appeared on October 15, 2015.

to which they are entitled by law, and by nature's sacred decree that human life is the offspring of two parents. The phrase, *the best interests of the child*, is used five times in the Divorce Act, twice in section 16, for court orders in custody and access, and thrice in section 17, that varies, rescinds, or suspends orders. This phrase tracks the court's orders.

My friends, now to this legal phrase's pedigree in the common law and in the ancient British sovereign King's law, the *lex prerogativa*, as the supreme guardian of children, the *parens patriae*. Long ago, the King delegated this power to the highest judge after himself, the Lord Chancellor, the Keeper of the Great Seal, and the Keeper of the King's conscience. In his ancient Courts of Chancery and Equity, the Lord Chancellor exercised this unique jurisdiction to protect children and the vulnerable in equity. Later, his courts acquired the powers of the King's Courts of Wards and Liveries. These originated when the children of knights killed in the King's service became wards of the King, who protected them and their property, delivered to them on their maturity. Later still, by the 1873 union of the common law, chancery and equity courts, all high and superior court judges, as child guardians, were endowed with these high equity powers.

My friends, the *parens patriae* is the ancient, but extant, power of the Queen as the country's supreme parent and children's guardian. *Black's Law Dictionary*, sixth edition, defines it at page 1114:

> *Parens patriae originates from the English common law where the King had a royal prerogative to act as guardian to persons with legal disabilities such as infants.*[10]

Jowitt's Dictionary o/English Law, 1959, volume 2, also defines it, at page *1294:*

> *The sovereign, as parens patriae, has a kind of guardianship over various classes of persons, who, from their legal disability,*

---

[10] Black's Law Dictionary, sixth edition, St. Paul, Minn.: W est Publishing Co., 1990, p. 1114

stand in need of protection, such as infants, idiots, and lunatics.[11]

Jowitt's volume 1 explains equity, at page 726:

... equity acts in personam; equity acts on the conscience; equity will not suffer a wrong to be without a remedy; equity follows the law; equity looks to the intent rather than the form; equity looks on that as done which ought to be done; equity imputes an intent to fulfill an obligation; equitable remedies are discretionary; delay defeats equities; he who comes to equity must come with clean hands;...[12]

The courts of chancery and equity were from time immemorial when literacy was rare hut vital, and the clerics, ecclesiastics, were literate, and Lord Chancellors were chosen from them. These literates and their literate clerks managed and recorded legal process, hence the terms *chancery, chancellor,* and *clerk* or *master* in chancery.

My friends, I come now to Canada's chancery courts and their powers for children. Upper Canada's 1837 *Act to Establish a Court of Chancery* in this Province enacted this court with powers for children like in Britain. This Act, section II, read, at page 765:

And be it further enacted by the authority aforesaid, That the said Court shall have jurisdiction, and possess the like power and authority as by the laws of England are possessed by the Court of Chancery in England, in respect of the matters hereinafter enumerated, that is to say: . . . in all matters related to infants, ideots and lunatics, and their estates,....[13]

---

[11] Jowitt's Dictionary of English Law, Vol. 2, London: Sweet & Maxwell Ltd., 1959, p.1294

[12] Jowitt's Dictionary of English Law, Vol. 1, London: Sweet & Maxwell Ltd., 1959, p.726

[13] An Act to establish a Court of Chancery in this Province, March 4, 1837, The Statutes of Upper Canada, to the time of the Union., Vol. I - Public Acts,

Nova Scotia also had such court. Later, the Brits, by their 1873 *Supreme Court of Judicature Act*, merged their common law and equity courts. This union vested their superior and high courts and judges with the chancery courts' royal equity powers to protect children and their property. Their 1873 Act, section 25.(10.), said:

> *In questions relating to the custody and education of infants the Rules of Equity shall prevail[14].*

Equity is conscience. Like the Brits, the 1881 *Ontario Judicature Act* merged its chancery, common law, and equity courts. This vested the inherent chancery courts' equity powers for children in our high and superior courts and judges. Like the British Act, the Ontario Judicature Act sections 17.(9) and 17.(10) said:

> *(9) In questions relating to the custody and education of infants, the Rules of Equity shall prevail.*
>
> *(10) Generally in all matters not hereinbefore particularly mentioned, in which there is any conflict or variance between the Rules of Equity and the Rules of the Common Law with reference to the same matter, the Rules of Equity shall prevail[15].*

Toronto: Robert Stanton, Printer to the Queen's Most Excellent Majesty., 1843, c II, s II, p. 765

[14] Supreme Court of Judicature Act, 1873, August 5, 1873, The Public General Acts passed in the Thirty-Sixth and Thirty-Seventh Years of the Reign of Her Majesty Queen Victoria, London: George Edward Eyre and William Spottiswoode, Printer to the Queen's most Excellent Majesty, 1873, c 66, s 25. (10), p. 17

[15] The Ontario Judicature Act, 1881, Statutes of the Province of Ontario passed in the session held in the Forty- Fourth Year of the Reign of Her Majesty Queen Victoria, Toronto: John Notman, Printer to the Queen's most Excellent Majesty, 1881, c 5, s 17.(9), (10), pp. 23-24

Equity's rules in conscience prevail. The law for children is ancient and true, though rooted in children who owned property.

My friends, the legal phrase, the best interests of the child, was set out in the famous defining judgment in the 1893 child protection case, *Queen v. Gyngall*, delivered in Britain's Queen's Bench Division, Court of Appeal. This court, by the 1873 merger, had received the *parens patriae* and chancery's equity powers. In *Gyngall*, the child barely knew her poor birth mother, ever unable to care for her. Much bounced around, this 15 year old child of delicate health was thriving in Miss Gyngall's care, even training to be a teacher's aide. She strongly opposed her mother's efforts to reclaim her. The good judges knew and spoke with the child. They ordered the child to Gyngall.

Master of the Rolls, the great Lord Esher, the highest judge after the Lord Chancellor, led this brilliant judgment. About their court's jurisdiction, he wrote, at page 239:

> *But there was another and an absolutely different and distinguishable jurisdiction, which has been exercised by the Court of Chancery from time immemorial. That was not a jurisdiction to determine rights as between a parent and a stranger, or as between a parent and a child.* **It was a paternal jurisdiction, a judicially administrative jurisdiction, in virtue of which the Chancery Court was put to act on behalf of the Crown, as being the guardian of all infants, in the place of a parent, and as if it were the parent of the child, thus superseding the natural guardianship of the parent.** *The present case arises after the Judicature Act, and the proceedings are in the Queen's Bench Division. The effect of that Act is, as I have often said, not to invent a new jurisdiction or to create new rights, but to alter the mode of procedure; and, there having been before two independent jurisdictions, one common law and the other equity, the Act in effect provides that, if a person proceeds in the Queen's Bench Division under the common law jurisdiction, and it turns out that the case raises questions to which the Chancery jurisdiction is applicable, the Queen's Bench Division judges are not to send the suitor to a Chancery Court, but are to exercise the Chancery*

jurisdiction themselves.[16]

Lord Esher went on, at page 240:

In the case of In re Spence (1), Lord Cottenham, L.C., said: "I have no doubt about the jurisdiction. The cases in which this Court interferes on behalf of infants are not confined to those in which there is property.... This Court interferes for the protection of infants, qua infants, by virtue of the prerogative which belongs to the Crown as parens patriae, and the exercise of which is delegated to the Great Seal."[17]

Lord Esher said, at page 241:

How is that jurisdiction to be exercised? The Court is placed in a position by reason of the prerogative of the Crown to act as supreme parent of children, and must exercise that jurisdiction in the manner in which **a wise, affectionate, and careful parent would act for the welfare of the child.**[18]

Lord Esher added, at page 242:

Then we have the case of In re McGrath (2), in which Lindley, L.J., said: "... The dominant matter for the consideration of the Court is the welfare of the child. But the welfare of a child is not to be measured by money only, nor by physical comfort only. The word 'welfare' must be taken in its widest sense. The moral and religious welfare of the child must be considered as well as its physical well-being. Nor can the ties of affection be disregarded." The Court has to consider, therefore, the whole of the circumstances of the case, the

---

[16] Court of Appeal, The Queen v. Gyngall, [1893], Queen's Bench Division, May 17,18, 1893, p. 239

[17] Court of Appeal, The Queen v. Gyngall, [1893], Queen's Beoch Division, May 17,18, 1893, page 240.

[18] Ibid, p. 241

position of the parent, the position of the child, the age of the child, the religion of the child so far as it can be said to have any religion, and the happiness of the child.[19]

Then Lord Justice Kay said, at page 247:

... Lord Hardwicke, professing not to go upon guardianship and disclaiming wardship, puts it upon this: that the Court represents the King, as parens patriae.[20]

He added, at page 248:

*This statement of the jurisdiction shews that, arising as it does from the power of the Crown delegated to the Court of Chancery, **it is essentially a parental jurisdiction, and that description of it involves that the main consideration to be acted upon in its exercise is the benefit or welfare of the child.***[21]

In its "parental jurisdiction" the court distinguishes child from parent. Lord Justice Kay continues, at page 251:

So again and again in such cases, where the child was not of very tender years, the practice has been that the judge himself saw the child, not for the purpose of obtaining the consent of the child, but for the purpose, and as one of the best modes of, determining what was really for the welfare of the child.[22]

My friends, this 1893 case set the stage and tone for the 20th century's enriched legal-judicial approach to children as human persons with their own needs, distinct and separate from their parents.

In *Queen v. Gyngall*, Lord Justice Kay states, for the world and all humanity, the sensitive, well established, and most

---

[19] Ibid, pp. 242 - 243

[20] Ibid, p. 247

[21] Ibid, p. 248

[22] Ibid, p. 251

famous words about the law on children, that, at page 252:

> *the superintending power in respect of infants, which Lord Eldon said the*
>
> *Court of Chancery had always exercised by delegation from the Crown as parens patriae, must be exercised as the Court may think for the best interests of the child.*[23]

This phrase is the conscience, humanity, and judicial power of the Sovereign and the state.

My friends, Liberal Minister MacGuigan and his successor, Progressive Conservative Crosbie, planted this judicial phrase *the best interests of the child* and its pedigree in the divorce law lexicon to clarify and express court and judicial duties to divorce's children. This phrase embodies and expresses the law that recognizes the child as an individual human person with rights, like Janusz Korczak's concept that children are complete beings from birth. It is a common mistake to unite the child's interests with one or both parents. *Gyngall* and like cases set out and put forth the law expressing the individual and complete child's humanity. Mindful of the harsh conditions in which children toiled, this 1893 legal framework *the best interests of the child* is one of the great gifts of the English high court judges to the common law world. In the 1890s, when child welfare was emerging, one writer noted that, in one night on a Toronto street, he counted 700 children, ragamuffins, street urchins, street arabs, begging and scrounging.

Pioneer Ministers MacGuigan and Crosbie enshrined children's positive rights in the federal divorce law, distinct from the provincial child protection laws. The child is its own person, with unique needs that include adult parental care. Its legal disabilities are privileges that vest adults with duties to them. It is, as this vulnerable separate being, that the child needs the love and care of its two parents.

My friends, I come now to the defining 1925 American judgment in the New York Court of Appeal. The case is

---

[23] Ibid, p. 252

Finlay v. Finlay, wherein Justice Benjamin Cardozo applied *Queen v. Gyngall.* In judgment, he wrote, at page 938:

> *The jurisdiction of a state to regulate the custody of infants found within its territory does not depend upon the domicile of the parents. It has its origin in the protection that is due to the incompetent or helpless.*[24]

The clear-minded Justice Cardozo invoked the Lord Chancellor's common and equity law jurisdiction. He cited *Gyngall,* at page 940:

> *The chancellor in exercising his jurisdiction upon petition does not proceed upon the theory that the petitioner, whether father or mother, has a cause of action against the other or indeed against anyone. He acts as parens patriae to do what is best for the interest of the child.* **He is to put himself in the position of a "wise, affectionate, and careful parent" (Reg. v. Gyngall, supra),** *and make provision for the child accordingly. He may act at the intervention or on the motion of a kinsman, if so the petition comes before him, but equally he may act at the instance of anyone else.* **He is not adjudicating a controversy between adversary parties, to compose their private differences. He is not determining rights "as between a parent and a child," or as between one parent and another.**[25]

Justice Cardozo explains equity, at page 940:

> He *"interferes for the protection of infants, qua infants, by virtue of the prerogative which belongs to the Crown as parens patriae."* . . . **The plaintiff makes no pretense of invoking this paternal jurisdiction.... He invokes the jurisdiction of a court to settle a dispute. Equity**

[24] Court of Appeals of New York, *Finlay v. Finlay,* 240 N.Y. 429; 148 N.E. 624; 1925 N.Y. Lexis 748; 40 A.L.R. 937, July 15, 1925, p. 938

[25] Ibid, p. 940

does not concern itself with such disputes in their relation to the disputants. Its concern is for the child[26].

Equity's concern is the child. These two judgments, *Gyngall* and *Finlay*, clarified the law in child cases that the high court judges' duty is not to adjudicate or settle disputes between the parents. It is to protect and decide the best interests of the child in the circumstances.

My friends, now to Canada's Supreme Court's 1993 judgment, *Young v. Young*. Madame Justice Claire L'Heureux-Dube dissented, concurred in by two other justices. About access parents, she wrote, at page 7:

The role of the access parent is that of a very interested observer, giving love and support to the child in the background.[27]

About the custodial parent, she said, at page 41:

The need for continuity generally requires that the custodial parent have the autonomy to raise the child as he or she sees fit without interference with that authority by the . . . non-custodial parent.[28]

About the non-custodial parent, she said, at page 47:

...the non-custodial spouse with access privileges is a passive bystander who is excluded from the decision-making process in matters relating to the child's welfare, growth and development.[29]

---

[26] Ibid, p. 940

[27] Supreme Court Judgements, *Young* v. *Young,* [1993]4 SCR 3, File No. 22227, January 25, 1993, p. 7

[28] Ibid, p. 41

[29] Ibid, p. 47

About men, she said, at page 49:

> ...*men as a group have not yet embraced responsibility for child care.*[30]

Queen's University Law Professor, Nicholas Bala, in his 1995 article, *In the Best Interests of the Child*, published in the Supreme Court Law Review, wrote on *Young v. Young*. About this Justice, he wrote, at page 455-56:

> *Justice L'Heureux-Dube . . . wrote a lengthy dissenting judgment in which she emphasized that the best interests of the child are served by protecting the position of the custodial parent.*[31]

He said, at page 461:

> *As in her 1992 spousal support judgment in Moge v. Moge, she offers an explicitly feminist analysis, discussing social science literature about gendered child care roles in marriage and after separation.*[32]

Madame Justice's words jolt the sensibilities. Equity knows only the law and conscience. It knows no social science literature, nor of non-custodial parent as bystanders. *The best interests of the child*, as law and equity, are not open to private views. The jurisprudence is clear that the judges' concern is the child, not the parents' conflict, nor their gender, nor gender roles. Justice Sopinka said the opposite, at page 15, that:

> *The best interests of a child are more aptly served by a law which recognizes the right of that child to a meaningful post-divorce relationship with both parents. The "rights" must be distributed between the custodial and the access parent so as to encourage such*

---

[30] Ibid, p. 49

[31] Bala, Nicholas, The Best Interests of the Child, The Supreme Court Law Review, 1995, Vol. 6 (2d), pp. 455 -"456

[32] Ibid, p. 461

a relationship[33].

The best interests of the child legal framework is in the Divorce Act to strengthen the court and the judges' duties to divorce's children. For a while, family and divorce law were afflicted by divisive ideological debate. Clearly, when family relations are tense and difficult, divorce proceedings are poor forums for such debate. It is also clear that badly drafted statutes will plunge all into muddy waters. For this, *the best interests of the child* was entrenched in the Act, to give judges strong tools to do what they are constituted to do, in judicial independence and in their royal duty to uphold children, despite spousal dispute.

My friends, innocent children must not pay for history's sins. Ideology claims place heavy burdens on judges, who are neither family counsellors nor magicians. The law *the best interests of the child* decrees that judges be just. As the most complete and authentic legal tool affirming children's rights, *the best interests of the child* is not poetry, nor a well-intended, earnest expression of humanity. It is the law of a "Judicially administrative jurisdiction," exercised exclusively by the judges in their ken, the courts, in their court orders. But its fate and future lay in the legislative ken, parliament, and provincial assemblies which enact laws. I thank you all for your   attention.

---

[33] Supreme Court Judgements, Young v. Young, [1993]4 SCR 3, File No. 22227, January 25, 1993, p. 15

SPECIAL THANKS

With special thanks to Diana Davidson, Leland Dieno, and Dale Tournemille, without whom the book would be still-born in my mind.

Proof

Made in the USA
Charleston, SC
19 December 2016